Maynooth Studies in Local History

SERIES EDITOR Raymond Gillespie

This volume is one of six short books published in the Maynooth Studies in Local History series in 2018. Like their predecessors they range widely, both chronologically and geographically, over the local experience in the Irish past. Chronologically they span the worlds of medieval Tristernagh in Westmeath, a study of an early 19th-century land improver, the Famine of the 1840s in Kinsale, politics and emigration in the late 19th century and sectarian rituals in the late 19th and 20th centuries. Geographically they range across the length of the country from Derry to Kinsale and westwards from Westmeath to Galway. Socially they move from those living on the margins of society in Kinsale and Galway in the middle of the 19th century to the politics and economics of the middle class revealed in the world of Thomas Bermingham and the splits in Westmeath in the 1890s. In doing so they reveal diverse and complicated societies that created the local past, and present the range of possibilities open to anyone interested in studying that past. Those possibilities involve the dissection of the local experience in the complex and contested social worlds of which it is part as people strove to preserve and enhance their positions within their local societies. Such studies of local worlds over such long periods are vital for the future since they not only stretch the historical imagination but provide a longer perspective on the shaping of society in Ireland, helping us to understand the complex evolution of the Irish experience. These works do not simply chronicle events relating to an area within administrative or geographically determined boundaries, but open the possibility of understanding how and why particular regions had their own personality in the past. Such an exercise is clearly one of the most exciting challenges for the future and demonstrates the vitality of the study of local history in Ireland.

Like their predecessors, these six short books are reconstructions of the socially diverse worlds of the poor as well as the rich, women as well as men, the geographical marginal as well as those located near the centre of power. They reconstruct the way in which those who inhabited those worlds lived their daily lives, often little affected by the large themes that dominate the writing of national history. They also provide models that others can follow up and adapt in their own studies of the Irish past. In such ways will we understand better the regional diversity of Ireland and the social and cultural basis for that diversity. They, with their predecessors, convey the vibrancy and excitement of the world of Irish local history today.

Maynooth Studies in Local History: Number 136

The Parnell split in Westmeath: the bishop and the newspaper editor

Michael Nolan

FOUR COURTS PRESS

Set in 10pt on 12pt Bembo by
Carrigboy Typesetting Services for
FOUR COURTS PRESS LTD
7 Malpas Street, Dublin 8, Ireland
www.fourcourtspress.ie
and in North America for
FOUR COURTS PRESS
c/o IPG, 814 N Franklin St, Chicago, IL 60622

ISBN 978–1–84682–719–8

Printed in Ireland
by SprintPrint, Dublin.

Contents

Acknowledgments

M y thanks are due to the many individuals and institutions that assisted me in the preparation of this short book, and in the preparation of the thesis for the degree of MA in Irish history at Maynooth University, on which it is based. First, I would like to thank Professor Marian Lyons for her helpful guidance when I first set out to research this topic. Second, my thanks to my thesis supervisor, Professor Terence Dooley, not just for his insightful comments and helpful advice during the preparation of the thesis, but also for his assistance and encouragement in preparing this study for publication. Thanks are also due to Professor Raymond Gillespie for inviting me to contribute to this series and for his useful suggestions which have enhanced the quality of the work. I am grateful also for the assistance received from the staff of the various libraries and archives that I have consulted, including Maynooth University Library, Westmeath County Library, the National Library of Ireland, the National Archives of Ireland and Meath Diocesan Archives. I would like to acknowledge also the support received from my fellow MA students at Maynooth and thank them for their friendship. Finally, I would like to express my appreciation to my family for their help and encouragement in the preparation of this study.

The front cover image of the bishop's palace, Mullingar, is reproduced courtesy of the National Library of Ireland.

Introduction

The split in the Irish Parliamentary Party (IPP) in 1890 was caused by Parnell's insistence on remaining as leader of the party despite the opposition of the majority of his former colleagues. After the split, the party divided into two antagonistic groups pursuing a bitter struggle for supremacy on political platforms, in the meeting rooms of political organizations and local government bodies, and in the pages of the national and provincial newspapers. The crisis, which came after a period of unparalleled success for the nationalist movement, convulsed the whole country and divided local communities everywhere, with the bitterness and rancour that it created taking generations to heal. Although the split in the IPP was precipitated by the divorce case in which Parnell was named as co-respondent, there is ample evidence that it was the product also of deepening divisions within the party that predated the divorce crisis by several years. In Westmeath, the national issues were complicated by a particularly virulent dispute in Mullingar in the 1880s between the local Catholic bishop, Dr Thomas Nulty, and his clergy, and a group of politically involved townsmen led by newspaper editor, John P. Hayden, who were representative of a growing and more assertive Catholic middle class in the country. Following the split, this group of townsmen provided the leadership for the Parnellite side in the town and also to some degree in the county at large, until they were overcome by superior forces in which the bishop and the Catholic Church played leading roles.

While this period in Irish history has been the subject of numerous national studies, little attention has been paid to the Parnell crisis in this part of Ireland with the notable exceptions of A.C. Murray's 1986 article in *Irish Historical Studies* entitled 'Nationality and local politics in late nineteenth-century Ireland: the case of county Westmeath' and David Lawlor's 2007 book on the Parnell split in Meath: *Divine right? The Parnell split in Meath*. Murray's article deals with the Parnell split and the earlier dispute between Hayden and Nulty in the context of factional and class rivalry in local politics in Westmeath. Lawlor's book is a comprehensive study of the Parnell split in the neighbouring county of Meath, which was part of the same Catholic diocese as Westmeath, and in which Bishop Nulty, as bishop of the diocese, was also prominently involved.[1] This study seeks to add to the corpus of local history of the period by examining the Parnell crisis in Westmeath with particular emphasis on the role played by the two main protagonists, Bishop Nulty and newspaper editor, Hayden. Because the fractious relationship between the two had developed long before the split, the events of this earlier time are also examined because of their central importance in determining the subsequent course of the dispute in the county. While the divorce case was primarily a moral issue for the Church and this was the main plank of its opposition to Parnell, both nationally and in Westmeath, this study argues that the unprecedented campaign that it waged against Parnellism was an attempt at the same time to hold on to its declining position of leadership in Irish political life and counter the threat to that authority represented by the Parnellite opposition. This is not just the story of the struggle for supremacy between the Parnellites and their opponents in Westmeath; it is also the story of the struggle between the Church and a section of the Catholic middle class for the leadership of the nationalist movement in the county.

In comparison with its immediate neighbours, Westmeath in the late 19th century was a relatively prosperous county. The great majority of the county's population (73 per cent) lived on agricultural holdings, 40 per cent of which were in excess of £15 rateable valuation. While this proportion was lower than Meath, with its larger farms, it was still considerably greater than Roscommon and Longford, which had just 17 and 31 per cent respectively of holdings in this category.[2] The extent of grazing land in the county may have had a bearing on this prosperity, however, as Westmeath at the time had the second-highest proportion of its land under grass in the entire country, exceeded only by its near neighbour, Meath.[3] Notwithstanding its relative prosperity, the county, like most others, experienced a steady decline in population after the Famine. In 1891, the population stood at 65,109, a decrease of 9 per cent since the previous census 10 years earlier.[4] Many of those who emigrated were the non-inheriting sons and daughters of small farmers, who without a substantial dowry or a farm of their own had little prospect of marriage in a country where the numbers of those who never married were extraordinarily high.[5] Catholics made up the great majority of the county's population (92 per cent) but this was not reflected in their share of influence in the professional and public affairs of the county, where the much smaller Protestant population still enjoyed a role out of all proportion to their numbers.[6] Protestants were over-represented not just in the professions, but also in the higher ranks of the military and police, in public administration and particularly among the landlord class.[7] Nevertheless, there had been an inexorable decline in their influence in public affairs with this decline most evident in the parliamentary representation of the county, which until 1871 was dominated by the landed aristocracy, but at the time of this study had become the preserve of the Catholic middle class. The county, from 1885, was represented in the United Kingdom parliament by two MPs, one from each of the parliamentary divisions of North and South Westmeath. Before that, the county was a single constituency electing two MPs while the borough of Athlone was a separate constituency with one representative. Although the urban population of the county was relatively high compared with its neighbours, Westmeath contained just two towns with populations exceeding 1,500 people:

Mullingar and Athlone. These were the only towns in the county with local government structures, both having town commissioners elected by ratepayers.[8] The only equivalent representative bodies for the rural population were the poor law unions, which covered a much greater geographical area. Their boards of guardians consisted of equal numbers of *ex officio* and elected members, with the latter elected by those who paid the poor law rate, which included most tenant farmers. The poor law unions, while originally designed for the relief of the poor and destitute, had over time 'evolved into a broad-based welfare system encompassing poor relief, medical care, sanitation and social housing'.[9] Like the town commissioners, their elected members were, at the time of this study, dominated by nationalist politicians. Among the poor law unions that served the county, Mullingar, which lay entirely within the county boundaries, was by far the biggest. It was also among the richest in the country, in terms of rateable valuation per head, coming in tenth place out of the 160 unions in the country.[10] Mullingar was not only the headquarters of the poor law union but also of the county grand jury, an unelected body composed largely of the landed gentry, responsible mainly for the construction and upkeep of public roads. Mullingar, therefore, as the headquarters of the local government bodies, the place of publication of three newspapers and the principal market town of the county, was of prime importance in the public affairs of the county and in the lives of the great majority of its inhabitants.[11] For these reasons, and not least because the two key figures in the dispute, Nulty and Hayden, resided in the town, it dominates this account of the Parnell split in Westmeath.

Contemporary national and provincial newspaper records have provided the principal primary source material for this study.[12] Newspapers, and particularly the provincial press, played a crucial part in the lives of local communities in the late 19th century, a time when literacy levels were increasing rapidly.[13] They reported, often in considerable detail, the proceedings of the political associations, the local government bodies, the courts, as well as the election campaigns, and, as such, are a valuable record of the period and the political pronouncements of its public figures. Although the editorial comment of provincial newspapers was often biased and partisan and their news coverage highly selective, they provide, nevertheless, a valuable insight into the issues of the time and the way people thought about those issues. An extensive range of provincial papers served every part of the country, with many counties supporting more than one publication. Westmeath had no less than five weekly newspapers at this time: the *Westmeath Examiner*, *Westmeath Guardian* and *Westmeath Nationalist*, published in Mullingar, and the *Westmeath Independent* and *Athlone Times*, published in Athlone.[14] In addition to the provincial press, the national dailies also circulated widely, with the *Freeman's Journal*, because it was associated with the IPP, a particularly good source for the proceedings of the party, both at a national as well at a local level. Indeed, the accounts of the newspaper's reporters at the crucial meetings in Westminster, which decided the fate of Parnell's leadership, were used subsequently as the official minutes by the party.[15]

The Royal Irish Constabulary (RIC) intelligence reports are another valuable source for the history of this period and have also been used extensively in the preparation of this study. Mullingar was the headquarters of the midland division of the RIC whose area of responsibility included Meath and Westmeath as well as a number of other midland and western counties. In addition to its normal policing function, the RIC acted as the eyes and ears of the British administration, gathering intelligence on the activities of organizations considered a threat to the state, as well as reporting on key public figures of the time including political activists and churchmen. The information contained in the police files does need to be treated with caution, however, relying as it does not just on direct observation by police officers but on a network of informers who may have embellished the reports or put their own interpretation on the events they described. Despite these limitations, the police files contain a wealth of directly relevant information on the dispute and the key players within it.[16]

One of those key players was Bishop Nulty and one would have expected the Meath diocesan archives to yield much useful information on his role in the dispute. Unfortunately, the diocesan records from the time of the study were destroyed in 1909 by the then bishop, Dr Gaughran, and apart from a single letter, no private correspondence relating to Nulty's involvement in the dispute survives.[17] The reasons for the destruction remain unclear, but it is likely that some material in the archive had become for the church authorities what historian Alfred Smyth has called an 'embarrassing encumbrance'[18] and the decision was made to destroy the entire archive rather than run the risk that selective disclosure might cause scandal among the laity.[19] Despite the destruction of the archive it is still possible to piece together Nulty's participation in the dispute in considerable detail from the many printed contemporary records that are still available. The diocesan archives contain a number of bound volumes consisting mainly of published pamphlets of Nulty's speeches and pastoral letters, some of which relate to the political controversies in which he was involved.[20] He did, of course, make many other public pronouncements from the pulpit and elsewhere and these were recorded in the local newspapers and in some cases in the national newspapers as well.

Hayden's pulpit was the *Westmeath Examiner*, and the newspaper archive holds the record of his views, or at least those intended for public consumption. It charts his political development through his speeches and writings, from his earliest beginnings as a local councillor in Mullingar, though the acrimony of the Parnell split, to his emergence on the national stage as MP for South Roscommon. Like Nulty, none of his personal correspondence survives, except for a small number of carefully chosen records relating mainly to his efforts to have the proscriptions that Nulty placed on the reading of the *Examiner* lifted. These records are now in the Meath diocesan archives. A note in the archives relates that, before he died, Hayden destroyed a great number of records from this period and it seems likely that he did not want the dispute between himself and the Church from those far off days to tarnish his reputation at a time when Church power and influence in independent Ireland was at its zenith. This is borne out by what is the perhaps the most interesting of the Hayden records in the diocesan archives: an unpublished memoir of his political career, compiled not long before his death and which is remarkable for the absence of any reference to the controversies involving Nulty and himself.[21]

The story of the Parnell split in Westmeath is told in chronological sequence, with the first chapter, 'The gathering storm', ranging from the Land War up to the split in the party in December 1890. This was the time when, after a period of unprecedented success in relation to land reform and political influence at Westminster, dissention appeared in the nationalist movement at national level and at local level in Westmeath also, where Nulty quelled a challenge to his authority in Mullingar only to see it re-emerge on a much larger scale after the divorce verdict. This challenge, which came from a small group of young politically involved men in Mullingar led by John Hayden, was representative of a growing middle-class revolt in relation to the dominant role of the Catholic Church in politics. The second chapter, 'A fight to the finish', extends from the walkout by a majority of the party in committee room 15 in the House of Commons to Parnell's death in October in the following year. It describes how the split in the party developed into all-out warfare, both in the country and in Westmeath, with both sides pitted against each other in an increasingly bitter dispute, fuelled by a partisan press and an even more partisan Church. The death of Parnell did not end the dispute and it continued with renewed vigour as both sides hoped that the general election of 1892 would mark a turning point in their respective campaigns. The election when it came was a turning point, for one side at least, resulting in a decisive victory for the anti-Parnellites and a crushing defeat for their opponents. It is noteworthy also for the unprecedented intervention of Bishop Nulty in the election campaign, an intervention that was to have serious consequences for the bishop himself and for the reputation of the Church in his diocese. The third chapter, 'The verdict of the people', tells the story of this phase of the dispute, which lasted from the death of Parnell to the general election of 1892, at which time Parnellism as a political movement was effectively extinguished in Westmeath. The study concludes with a fourth chapter, 'The aftermath', which describes briefly the political landscape in the county following the dispute and the efforts made by the bishop to restore his reputation and that of his clergy in the remaining years of his life. It relates also how Hayden experienced something of a political rebirth after the death of Nulty and went on to become a leading figure in the politics of Westmeath in the early years of the new century.

1. The gathering storm

The decade of the 1880s leading up to the Parnell split was a time of great change in Ireland. The Land War (1879–82) that opened the decade had politicized a whole generation of the Irish population, not just farmers but town dwellers as well. This emergent class of educated townsmen rallied in support of the farmers, for reasons of self-interest – their livelihood depended on the prosperity of their country cousins – but also for reasons of self-fulfilment. They were a community whose time had come and they wanted to play an active part in the nationalist movement, particularly now that the prospect of home rule with its spoils of office loomed on the horizon. They faced one formidable obstacle, however, in the presence of the Catholic clergy who had long regarded themselves as the leaders of the Catholic community – not just in a spiritual sense but in temporal matters as well – and were not prepared to cede their powerful position to a lay leadership no matter how worthy their cause. The decade leading up to the Parnell split was to see this lay leadership increasingly assert itself at the expense of their clerical counterparts, with the period of the split itself marking a fight to the finish between a section of this leadership and a united Church which marshalled all of its forces against them. Nowhere was this more evident than in Mullingar where the dispute between John P. Hayden and his followers and the local bishop and his clergy, ostensibly in relation to the provision of a water supply to the town, increasingly developed into a struggle for supremacy in local politics between the two sides, a dispute that was to add immeasurably to the bitterness of the Parnell split in the county.

Despite A.C Murray's assertion that in the Land War 'Westmeath had been relatively quiet; [and] there had been little enthusiasm for the Land League'[1], the county recorded 16 Land League demonstrations in 1880 alone, in comparison with just 10 and 11 for its neighbours, Meath and Longford respectively.[2] In December 1880, for example, the crowd at a Land League meeting in Mullingar was estimated at over 10,000 while a similar meeting in Castlepollard in January of the following year attracted 12,000.[3] The League, a mass movement that had its origins in the west of Ireland, aimed to secure reductions in rents for farmers and ultimately ownership of the land they worked as tenants. It proved to be remarkably successful in its aims, even if the goal of full ownership of the land by the tenant farmers took some time to come to fruition. Intended as a peaceful movement for change, it led inevitably to a degree of intimidation and violence. Westmeath was the scene of one of the worst outrages of the period

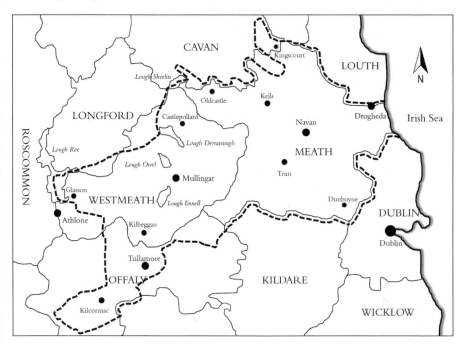

1. Map of Irish midlands with Catholic diocese of Meath highlighted

when, in April 1882, assassins targeting the landlord of the Barbavilla estate near Collinstown in the north of the county murdered the landlord's sister-in-law by mistake. Despite the barbarity of the killing, there was widespread sympathy in the local community for the 11 men who were eventually convicted of the murder, with one of their number, William Mc Cormack, a Land League member and substantial farmer, nominated and returned unopposed to Delvin poor law board of guardians while detained in Mullingar prison awaiting trial.[4]

Bishop Nulty was a strong supporter of the Land League; his support was a natural progression for a prelate with a long history of involvement in the struggle for tenant rights going back over many decades. His involvement was a product both of his background as the son of a tenant farmer and of his own personal experience of the horrors of the Famine, which he saw at first-hand while serving as a young priest.[5] Although Nulty, who had been bishop of the diocese since 1866, had written before of the plight of tenant farmers and their exploitation at the hands of the landlords, it was his much-quoted 1881 pamphlet, first published as a series of newspaper articles, that brought him to national and indeed international attention. In it, he wrote that the land of every country is the gift of its Creator to the people of that country; it is the patrimony and inheritance bequeathed to them by their Common Father, out of which they can by continuous labour and toil provide themselves with everything they require for their maintenance and support, and for their material comfort and enjoyment.

In what appeared to be a clear statement in favour of land nationalization (also advocated by Land League leader Michael Davitt) he maintained:

that no individual or class of individuals can hold a right of private property in the land of a country; that the people of that country, in their public corporate capacity, are, and always must be, the real owners of the land of their country.[6]

This was a radical view, particularly coming from a Catholic prelate, and Henry George, an American social reformer who held somewhat similar views to Nulty, wrote later that the English press was reporting his essay 'as an outrageous official declaration of Communism from a Catholic bishop'.[7] Gabriel Flynn, who has made a study of Nulty's involvement in the land agitation argued that, instead of nationalization, the bishop favoured a peasant proprietorship as a solution to the land issue.[8] It may be, however, that Nulty became reconciled to this view when it became apparent that nationalization had no prospect of being realized in the conservative economic climate of the time and more importantly, perhaps, found little favour with the tenant farmers who aspired to own the land themselves.[9] Nulty, nonetheless, was universally respected among all classes in the county and as yet there was little or no tension between himself and the nationalist movement in which he and his priests enjoyed privileged positions. He was moreover a fervent supporter of Parnell, who was president of the Land League, and took some pride in the fact that he was the first Irish bishop to support Parnell when he campaigned successfully for election to Parliament, for the constituency of Meath, in 1875.[10]

The Land War, which petered out in 1882 under the twin effects of government coercion on the one hand and concessions to tenant farmers on the other, was a godsend for Parnell who used it to assert his leadership of the nationalist movement at a critical time. Together with his party, which had profited handsomely from the land agitation, he lost no time in changing the direction of the movement, mobilizing the principal communities of interest to a common cause, which was the achievement of home rule by parliamentary means. For this he needed to gain the support of the Land League leadership and the organizational strength and countrywide reach of the Catholic clergy. The vehicle for this purpose was the Irish National League (INL); founded in late 1882 by Parnell, with Tim Harrington, later to become MP for Westmeath, as secretary. The INL, which replaced the Land League organization, was a great

2. Bishop Thomas Nulty
(courtesy of the National
Library of Ireland)

success and grew to a staggering total of 1,285 branches throughout the country
by mid-1886.[11] It was a success in Westmeath too, with a convention held in
Mullingar in October 1885, attended by representatives of 29 branches of the
organization in the county.[12]

As far as Parnell and his party were concerned, all the pieces of the jigsaw
had now come together. The clergy had diverted their energies to the new body
and used their formidable organizational skills to establish branches throughout
the country. Meanwhile, the old Land League leadership had transferred their
allegiance to the new organization, bringing with them the experience they
had gained in the cauldron of the land war. For the farmers, while the land acts
of 1881 and 1885 had brought considerable gains, they had at the same time
merely whetted their appetite for more concessions with the ultimate prize: full
ownership, on their terms, of the land they worked as tenants. The genius of
Parnell and his lieutenants was in convincing them that the pursuit of home rule
by parliamentary means was a better route to the fulfilment of their dreams, than
by the often-violent agitation, which was the practice heretofore. A measure of

the success of this changed strategy in Westmeath was the remarkable fall in the number of agrarian outrages recorded in the county, which fell from 131 in 1882 to just 20 a year later.[13] The value of the farmers to the nationalist movement was greatly enhanced by the Representation of the People Act 1884, which conceded the vote to all male householders and resulted in an increase in the Westmeath electorate from 3,799 in 1881–2 to 10,465 in 1891.[14] Although farm labourers had benefited also from the franchise reform, and the labourers acts of 1883 and 1885 had gone some way in addressing their perilous living conditions, this community – unlike the farmers – had little influence in the nationalist movement. While some of the nationalist leaders, including Parnell, were sympathetic to their plight, they attracted little sympathy from their farming cousins who stood only to lose from any amelioration of labourer conditions. In a rural county like Westmeath, the support of farmers was of prime importance to the nationalist movement and the achievement of Parnell and his party was to create an unprecedented unity in a common cause between them and the other influential communities that made up the nationalist population, namely: the shopkeepers and middle classes in the towns and, not least, the clergy. Indeed, Nulty was to highlight this harmony in the heart of his own diocese, when 'he referred with pleasure to the unity which now, as ever, exists among the priests and laity … nowhere in Ireland is that union firmer than here in Mullingar where priests, bishops, and people were all of one way of thinking'.[15]

This happy state of affairs in the county town was not to last, however, and the bishop himself was to be a prime mover in a local dispute that brought this exceptional degree of harmony to a rather undignified end. What started as a disagreement over the issue of a supply of water to the town developed into a battle of wills between the bishop and his clergy on the one hand, and a section of the townspeople on the other, for the leadership of the nationalist movement; a dispute that intensified in the lead up to the Parnell split and continued during the split and beyond.

The dispute would probably not have gained the notoriety that it did, nor lasted as long, but for the role of the local nationalist newspaper, the *Westmeath Examiner*. The *Examiner* was founded in 1882 by two brothers from Co. Roscommon, Luke and John Hayden. Luke, the older of the two by some 13 years, was the proprietor of the *Roscommon Messenger* and prominent in local politics in his native Roscommon, later becoming an MP in 1885. John was just 19 when he came to Mullingar to take over the running of the *Examiner* and soon became involved in the politics of his adopted town, becoming a committee member of the Mullingar branch of the INL when it was set up in November of the following year.[16] The launch of the *Examiner* in 1882 came at an opportune time for John as he set out on his political and professional journey. It provided him not just with a means of earning a living, but also with a platform to further his political ambitions now that the resurgent nationalist movement was entering a new phase in its campaign. The *Examiner*'s first edition set out the paper's principles:

> to keep alive and intensify the spirit of self-reliance which now pervades the people, to give greater facilities on all occasions for the free expression of the people's wishes, to so consolidate the popular opinions that they may be of most support to the Irish party, led by Mr Parnell. With this object we shall endeavour, by strict attention to local affairs, to assist in the education of the people in the art of self-government, show them what is to be gained by depending on themselves, and devoting their energies towards securing the management of their affairs in small as well as in great things.[17]

It was a manifesto perfectly attuned to the new era opening up in Irish politics under the leadership of Parnell, and Hayden as one of the new generation of young middle-class nationalists was poised to take advantage of the opportunities that that new era presented. He was to use the pages of his newspaper in the months and years ahead to proclaim his views fearlessly, not only on the political situation at a national level, but on local affairs as well.

The representatives on the local government bodies (Hayden was elected a Mullingar town commissioner in 1885) enjoyed the confidence of the bishop and the clergy, as long as they confined themselves to routine matters of local administration, and did not challenge the Church or its tacit leadership of the nationalist community. That it did not take much to cross the line into forbidden territory was demonstrated in early 1886 when the bishop reacted badly to Hayden and like-minded colleagues on the town commissioners backing a water scheme for the town of Mullingar. The scheme, proposed by the local poor law board, was opposed by Nulty.[18] The provision of a water supply to the town had long been debated by the poor law board and town commissioners. It was a contentious issue because of the considerable cost involved, which would fall on the ratepayers of the town in the form of increased rates. The bishop, unhappy with the scheme of the poor law board, proposed his own scheme that would involve supplying water to the town from a local river and using existing wells and pumping facilities in Church-owned property. Controversially, the scheme involved an annual charge to be paid by the poor law board, which Nulty maintained he planned to use to assist the education of poor children, thus relieving the ratepayers of the expense of maintaining such children in the workhouse.[19] The respect and reverence with which the bishop was held in the town meant that his waterworks scheme was not subjected to the detailed scrutiny that a project of its magnitude warranted and his proposal was unanimously adopted at a meeting of the board of guardians of the poor law union in September of 1886.[20] Opposition to Nulty's scheme was not just confined to Hayden and his colleagues; Lord Greville, who

3. John P. Hayden.

was the local landlord, also opposed it. While Dr Nulty claimed no jurisdiction over Protestants such as Lord Greville, it was different for Hayden who, as a Catholic, was expected to fall in with whatever the bishop proposed, even if it disadvantaged him and other ratepayers who had to foot the bill.

Hayden's opposition to the bishop's plan coincided with the high point of the IPP who secured 85 of the country's 103 parliamentary seats in the general election, which took place at the end of 1885, including the two Westmeath seats which they won with overwhelming majorities. The party candidates for the Westmeath seats were Donal Sullivan, a native of Co. Cork, whose only connection with the county was that his brother Timothy had previously served as an MP for Westmeath, and James Tuite, a Mullingar jeweller, who had been active in local politics for several years. Tuite, like Hayden, was one of the rising Catholic middle class, but unlike Hayden, he would remain loyal over the course of his political career to the Church's dominant role in the politics of the county. Tuite had served his political apprenticeship in the Land League, becoming secretary of the Mullingar branch, and had achieved the distinction (in the eyes of nationalists) of being imprisoned twice for his League activities.[21] He was a long-standing member of the Mullingar town commissioners and served for a number of years as chairman of that body. Both Tuite and Sullivan had been selected at a county convention presided over by a clerical chairman and in each case the candidates were proposed by local priests.[22] Despite appearances, however, the semblance of clerical control was merely illusory. As J.H. Whyte observed, already at this time the selection of the candidates was controlled by the party hierarchy, resulting in a situation where 'in the space of a few years the clergy had been completely elbowed out of one of the fields in which they had hitherto been supreme'.[23]

Thus, Hayden's rebellion, even if of a modest character, may have come at a time when the bishop and his clergy were unduly sensitive to the steady erosion of their power by the Catholic middle class. Another example of this heightened sensitivity from the same time was a perceived slight over the issue of payments to the county MPs, who at the time received no public funding. A committee established for this purpose, and with Hayden and his followers prominent among the organizers, made payments in 1884 and 1885 to the county members. The 1885 payment of £150 was presented to each MP in the offices of the *Westmeath Examiner* with only the executive committee present.[24] When the time came to organize the collection again the following year the bishop was no longer prepared to allow a lay committee, particularly one dominated by Hayden and his followers, to continue in control of the fund. Explaining that the clergy 'felt nettled' at their exclusion from the presentation in the previous year – not surprisingly, given that they had been centrally involved in organizing the collection at the church gates throughout the county – Nulty announced that they would not just collect the money but also make the presentation themselves.[25]

Events happening on the national stage at this time may also have given the bishop further cause for concern in relation to Hayden and his followers. In early 1886, Parnell had imposed Captain William O'Shea, the husband of his lover, as candidate for a by-election in Galway against the wishes of prominent members of his own party. The imposition of O'Shea created much bad feeling and marked a major turning point in the attitude of some party members towards their leader, with Callanan remarking that the debacle 'precipitated a deep rift in the Irish party which prefigured the split five years later'.[26] Parnell's liaison with Katharine O'Shea was common knowledge in the corridors of Westminster at the time and must have been widely known in Ireland too. It was a time when silence all round might have been the best option, in light of Parnell's motivation for supporting O'Shea. Nevertheless, Mullingar town commissioners with Hayden in the chair somewhat injudiciously adopted a resolution in support of Parnell in relation to the Galway election, an action that, in the circumstances, was hardly calculated to endear him or the commissioners to the bishop or his clergy.[27]

The first real trial of strength, however, between the two sides came later in the same year when, at a meeting of the Mullingar branch of the INL, a local priest acting on the bishop's behalf attempted to depose M.J. Halton,

one of Hayden's supporters, as president of the branch. The move was resisted
by Halton, resulting in a walkout by the priest and his supporters. Halton was
subsequently re-elected president by those that remained and a new rival branch
of the organization was established by the defectors.[28] However, the dispute
sucked the vitality out of both branches, with the result that by the following
summer 'both had ceased to hold regular meetings'.[29]

Meanwhile, further cracks in the edifice of the nationalist movement, at
leadership level, were appearing. Two of Parnell's most able lieutenants, William
O'Brien and John Dillon, introduced a new land agitation called the Plan of
Campaign in October 1886, which quickly attracted a resolute government
response in the form of a severe coercion act. The plan, launched in response
to worsening agricultural prices, had a mixed reception. Parnell himself stood
aloof, exacerbating the bad feeling lingering towards him from the Galway by-
election, while the bishops, with some notable exceptions, were supportive. It
was broadly supported in Westmeath too. Just six weeks after its introduction,
a large demonstration in the west of the county organized by the INL and
presided over by a local priest heard rousing speeches from the two county MPs,
Tuite and Sullivan, in support of the plan.[30] Nevertheless, there were concerns,
particularly at the flouting of the law which it entailed, which resulted in the
government, and even some of the bishops, complaining to Rome, resulting in
the plan being condemned by the pope in early 1888. The papal rescript, as it
was called, attracted a defiant response from Dillon who asserted in a speech
in Drogheda, 'that in the conduct of our national affairs ... we Irishmen –
Protestant and Catholic alike – all equal before the law, shall be free from any
interference whether it comes from Italy or any other country'.[31] The bishops,
in the circumstances, sensibly downplayed the papal rescript but they were
understandingly concerned with the challenge to the authority of the Church
that its rejection entailed, with the archbishop of Dublin, Dr Walsh, expressing
his fear privately that the country might 'well go the way of France and Italy'.[32]

Nevertheless, the Plan of Campaign did come at an opportune time
for Hayden, allowing him to flaunt his nationalist credentials when he was
under some pressure on his home turf. In September 1887, he was convicted
with a number of others, under the coercion act, of obstructing the police at
an eviction.[33] As he proclaimed himself in the *Examiner* not long after it was
established: 'for an Irishman' there was 'no surer road to the hearts of his
countrymen than the fact that he has been selected by the Government for
political prosecution or persecution'.[34] Demonstrating the truth of his dictum,
the conviction generated a groundswell of sympathy for him among the
population with a 'monster demonstration' at Tang, in the west of the county,
attracting no less than 11 priests as well as the two county MPs.[35] In Mullingar,
on the other hand, his martyr's status did not quite have the same effect and his
standing with the bishop and his clergy did not improve. In fact, on the day that
his appeal against his sentence was being heard, the town commissioners acting

4. and 5. Donal Sullivan (*left*) and James Tuite (*right*)
(both images courtesy of the National Library of Ireland)

at the behest of the clergy rejected Hayden as chairman by a majority vote. Shortly before Hayden's failed bid for the chairmanship, Dr Kerrigan, one of his supporters who was also opposed by the clergy, failed in his bid for re-election to the commissioners by a narrow margin.[36] Hayden duly served his sentence in Tullamore Jail, and while the *Examiner* did its best to drum up support for him by proclaiming that 'he [Hayden] accepts the rigour of his lot as the price of his patriotism, and is willing to pay it twice, thrice, aye, a hundred times over in the same cause',[37] his homecoming just after Christmas was low-key and ignored by the majority of the people and the priests.[38] The local MP, James Tuite, who had supported Hayden at the demonstration in Tang a few months earlier, was not so brave when it came to the bishop's home town and was conspicuous by his absence, sensibly deciding, as Murray observed, that 'it would be political suicide to oppose his patron the bishop'.[39] His colleague, the MP for South Westmeath, Donal Sullivan, was also wary of associating himself with Hayden. However, not living in the same town as the bishop, he could afford to hedge his bets and sent a letter apologizing for his non-attendance.[40]

Hayden was arrested again in January 1888 for a speech he made after he was released from prison. As on the previous occasion, his arrest and incarceration did nothing to soften the hearts of his opponents. In fact, while Hayden was in prison for the second time, Nulty decided to go on the offensive and proclaimed the reading of the *Examiner* as 'dangerous to the members of his flock'.[41] This latest action by the bishop was a serious escalation of the dispute and a commercial threat to the *Examiner*, particularly as Hayden's friend and supporter, M.J. Halton, claimed people were inferring from the bishop's remarks that 'it [was] a sin to read the paper'. There was no time to lose and Hayden's response was immediate, coming in the form of an appeal (by Halton in the absence of Hayden in prison) to the Metropolitan of the diocese of Meath, Archbishop Logue of Armagh – Nulty's nominal superior – asking him to intervene in the dispute.[42] Logue spoke to Nulty attempting to effect 'some kind of compromise' between him and Hayden, but Nulty 'would make no concession in the matter'. The Archbishop concluded that, from his own enquires, there was some justification for the action Nulty had taken and consequently 'any steps [he] could take in the matter would be a mere waste of time'.[43] If Logue was prepared to let the matter rest there, Nulty was not, following up his condemnation of the *Examiner* with an extraordinary attack on Hayden and his supporters. He castigated them as a 'socially [and] ... numerically insignificant' group, consisting, 'of six individuals, three of whom are wholly illiterate, whilst the other three have just picked up the amount of smattering, fragmentary knowledge that makes men arrogant and self-conceited, but does not make them educated or cultured'.[44] His outburst was all the more remarkable, considering that Hayden's followers included: Dr Kerrigan, who was a poor law guardian as well as county coroner, N.J. Downes, who was solicitor to the poor law board, M.J. Cleary, a Mullingar veterinary surgeon, and Hayden's intermediary with Archbishop Logue, M.J. Halton, a music teacher in the town and secretary of the local branch of the INL. Nulty was not only the acknowledged leader of the nationalist community in the town, but a man of considerable intellect also. The contemptuous tone of his remarks indicates not just a degree of personal affront that anyone should challenge his authority on any matter, regardless of its nature, but a disdain for those – particularly Hayden – whom he regarded as his intellectual inferiors. This is all too evident from his scathing reference to the *Examiner*, which he made at the same time and in which he commented: 'I never read a paragraph in the *Westmeath Examiner* that from a literary point of view seemed to me to rise above the level of a national school boy's essay'.[45] While Hayden, by proclaiming in the *Examiner* that 'no man, or no class of men are by virtue of their office and position constituted by that one fact alone leaders of the people in affairs not connected with the office',[46] was not saying anything different to what Dillon was saying on the national stage, he was regarded with much less tolerance by Church leaders such as Nulty. The bishop, while relatively powerless to challenge the insubordination to Church authority engendered by the Plan of Campaign, was determined to stamp out any nascent challenge to his authority on his own patch, particularly when that challenge came from those he regarded with the contempt that his remarks suggest.

A further opportunity for the bishop presented itself in October, when Nulty and his clergy in Mullingar orchestrated a successful campaign against Hayden's re-election to the town commissioners. Despite the weight of the opposition ranged against him, Hayden gained the support of more than 40 per cent of the electorate, indicating a level of support among the most influential of the town's citizens that cannot but have disturbed his opponents.[47] The Mullingar poor law guardians were already at this stage firmly in the bishop's camp and staunch supporters of his waterworks scheme, yet their support could not save it. Following rejection by the local government board who, at their inquiry in May 1888, heard that the guardian's waterworks committee reports had been prepared by the bishop himself 'and adopted at the board without alteration',[48] Nulty finally threw in the towel and withdrew his scheme the following year.[49]

The first public sign of the looming split appeared at the end of 1889 when Captain O'Shea filed for divorce on the grounds of his wife's adultery and named Parnell as co-respondent. While many in the party must have regarded the news as a portent of looming disaster, there was little public reaction. The nationalist population including the Church preferred to turn a blind eye, with many believing that it was just another move designed to damage Parnell and from which he would emerge triumphant, as he had done from the accusations that he had been implicated in the notorious Phoenix Park murders which occurred in the early part of the decade.[50] Parnell himself encouraged this attitude by 'repeated assurances to anyone who dared to beard him on the subject that all would come right in the end'.[51] Meanwhile, in Westmeath, as elsewhere in the country, the divorce case was ignored and an uneasy peace reigned. In the elections for Mullingar poor law board of guardians held the following March, the bishop's nominees were returned unopposed.[52] The same consensus did not obtain in the town commissioners, however, and in October Hayden and Kerrigan were successfully opposed by the clergy in their bid to be elected.[53] What relative state of calm existed in the country was to be shattered in November when a divorce decree, uncontested by Parnell, was granted to Captain O'Shea with the court proceedings extensively covered in the *Freeman's Journal*.[54] No member of the party, therefore, could say they were not aware of the significance of the decree. Nevertheless, just three days later a meeting of the party in Dublin passed a resolution of support for Parnell, which, significantly, was seconded by Tim Healy, who would later become one of his most vituperative opponents. On the same day, the Mullingar poor law guardians declared their support. Donal Sullivan, the MP for South Westmeath, came out strongly for Parnell also, declaring somewhat histrionically that following a recent visit to his constituency, he could say that both in the north and in the south of that county; the desire of the people was that, come weal come woe, as long as he had the honour to represent Westmeath, he should fight by the side of their great leader and should never falter in his ranks.[55]

These were sentiments that he would repudiate just a few short weeks later. The other Westmeath MP, James Tuite, also came out in support, but Nulty and his fellow bishops were more circumspect, preferring instead to sit and wait and see how events would unfold.[56] A party meeting later in the month re-elected Parnell as leader, unaware that the leader of the Liberal Party, William Gladstone, on whom the nationalists had pinned their hopes for home rule, had come out against his continued leadership of the party on moral grounds. This placed in jeopardy the holy grail of Irish nationalism and forced a re-appraisal of the support for Parnell. When the bishops finally declared against Parnell on 3 December 1890, during the protracted meeting of the party on the issue of his leadership in committee room 15, the die was cast and the disastrous split in the party occurred three days later.

2. A fight to the finish

The decision of the bishops to oppose Parnell and to enter the fight against him was to have profound repercussions for the nationalist struggle and also, perhaps most importantly from their own point of view, for their relationships with their flocks. Although there had been increasing tensions between the Catholic middle class – which dominated the nationalist movement – and the bishops in the period leading up to the split, this was the first time that a considerable body of the laity came out in organized opposition to the Church hierarchy. For the bishops, Parnell's continued leadership of the party, while primarily a moral issue, was a political issue as well. He had transgressed the code of morality that the bishops were obliged to uphold and his refusal to give way placed the cause of home rule and all the advances that had been made in support of the tenant farmers in jeopardy. In addition, and perhaps the most important if unspoken consideration for the bishops, was the fact that the support for Parnell, coming as it did after a decade of the steady erosion of their position of influence in Irish political life, represented an unprecedented rebellion by a section of the laity against their authority that they had little choice but to resist. Furthermore, the zeal with which they conducted their campaign suggests that they suspected 'that this was their last chance to restore their now-rapidly waning authority in political matters'.[1] Bishop Nulty provided a revealing insight into the Church's thinking at this time when he observed in relation to the Parnellite revolt 'that no national movement ever yet took place that had not at its head the bishops and priests of the country'.[2] Viewed from this perspective, there was no room for compromise and the Church's opposition, conducted in conjunction with the anti-Parnellite majority of the party, was unrelenting and in the end successful in its aim of defeating Parnellism and its support base – but at considerable cost to both the party and the Church. Because of the active involvement of Bishop Nulty, the campaign was prosecuted with particular diligence in Westmeath, where the dispute was given an added edge by the participation of the bishop's old enemy John P. Hayden on the Parnellite side.

For Hayden, who had long been a thorn in the side of Nulty and his clergy, it was a natural progression to the Parnellite cause. Ever the opportunist politician, he would have welcomed the chance to re-enter the political fray, having been banished from local politics by the actions of the bishop and his clergy. Parnell's cause, furthermore, was one with which he could readily identify; a leader condemned by the bishops and deserted by his erstwhile friends. Parnell's rallying cry of independence, not just from the Liberal party, but from clerical dictation as well, would have struck a chord with the young newspaper editor who had been proclaiming his own freedom to act as he thought fit in political affairs over many years in the pages of the *Westmeath Examiner*. As a newspaper man he had another reason to welcome the struggle that was enfolding; a political controversy with elements of tragedy can only have boosted newspaper sales, and the Parnell affair, in its early stages at least, was a big story. The *Athlone Times* reflected the prevailing mood when it reported 'nothing but Parnell and his party can be seen in the newspapers or talked of anywhere'.[3] The downside for Hayden was the considerable risk he was taking for his business by joining the battle against the formidable forces of the Church and the party majority. But he may have felt that he had little to lose in any event since the *Examiner* was already on the bishop's blacklist, and he might even benefit from the support of Parnellites, who may have been inclined in the past to shun his paper because of the bishop's strictures. In addition, Hayden and his small band of followers would no longer be an isolated dissenting minority in Mullingar but would in future be bolstered by the much larger numbers prepared to nail their colours to the Parnellite mast and assert their independence from Church control of nationalist politics. The Parnell crisis, therefore, while it was an undeniable threat to his business, was an opportunity also for Hayden to broaden his horizons as a politician and to make his mark on a wider stage. With his boundless energy and the *Examiner* as his mouthpiece, he was to provide much of the leadership of the Parnellite campaign then unfolding, not just in Mullingar but in the county at large.

The hierarchy's condemnation of Parnell on 3 December 1890 was the rallying call for the nationwide campaign against him and an encouragement for any wavering members of the party to abandon him in committee room 15, just three days later. The bishops' delay in making their statement led to accusations from the Parnellites that it was pragmatism rather than principle that guided their decision, as they had waited to make their pronouncement until the party changed direction following Gladstone's intervention. Nulty himself lent some credence to these claims when he seemed to suggest later that a temporary suspension of Parnell's leadership might have offered a solution to the bishops' dilemma; 'had Mr Parnell quietly withdrawn from public life for 12 months and made some apology to the people ... things would not be so bad for Ireland today'.[4] Furthermore, the fact that Nulty did not endorse the hierarchy's declaration until a day after it was issued encouraged speculation that he was a closet supporter of Parnell.[5] Tim Harrington MP was to follow up on this speculation some months later when he stated at a public meeting in Mullingar, attended by Parnell, that Nulty told Tim Healy in the wake of the divorce case verdict 'that Mr Parnell was the only man for Ireland'. Both Nulty and Healy later denied Harrington's assertion.[6]

Nevertheless, the hierarchy's intervention was decisive and the two Westmeath MPs, Tuite and Sullivan, joined the majority against him, despite

6. Charles Stewart Parnell
(courtesy of the National Library of Ireland).

their previous declarations of support, rightly calculating that the public mood would change following the bishops' intervention in the debate. Hayden was quick to denounce the MPs' actions in the *Examiner* as did the Mullingar poor law guardians and the town commissioners, but the MPs' decision, not surprisingly, brought a more favourable response from the clergy. Revd Edward O'Reilly of Mullingar, chairman of the local branch of the INL, was first off the mark in endorsing the MPs' decision, followed soon after by another prominent political priest, the Revd R.J. Kelsh the parish priest of Killucan. However, others were slower to take sides. Collinstown and Fore INL with the local parish priest Revd John Curry presiding, passed a resolution merely deploring the disunity in the party and expressing the hope that 'all Irish nationalists will reunite under any leader the Irish representatives may elect and the Irish people may approve of '.[7] In contrast to his counterpart in Ardagh and Clonmacnois, Dr Woodlock, who came out against Parnell in early December, Nulty waited until just before Christmas before strongly condemning Parnell to his congregation at Sunday mass in Mullingar, a further indication that the decision to declare against him had been a particularly painful one for the bishop.[8]

In the country in general, the Parnellites got a head start on their opponents. This was due, not just to the tardiness of the bishop's response, but also because of the Parnellite control of both the INL and the party funds and the support they enjoyed from the main nationalist daily, the *Freeman's Journal* and the party paper *United Ireland*. The importance of newspaper support to the Parnellites was highlighted in the immediate aftermath of the split when Parnell moved promptly to assert his control over *United Ireland* after it had initially sided with his opponents. In Westmeath, in addition to the *Examiner*, which came out week after week with leading articles eulogising Parnell and denouncing his opponents, the Parnellites also enjoyed the backing of the *Westmeath Independent*. The *Independent* famously incurred the wrath of Bishop Woodlock, when it compared Parnell's ordeal at the hands of his former supporters to Christ's treatment before his crucifixion. In a letter to the archbishop of Dublin, Woodlock wrote:

> the *Westmeath Independent* has an abominably blasphemous leading article today ... it says of the wretched adulterer: 'Who two days before was lauded to the skies', is now 'tortured and spat upon, until the recollection of the entry into Jerusalem and the crown of thorns forced itself vividly before our minds.' Is it not abominable?[9]

The Protestant-owned *Westmeath Guardian* on the other hand was much less polemical than either the *Independent* or the *Examiner*, although it had for a number of years reported extensively on Catholic and nationalist affairs in an apparent attempt to attract Catholic readers who had abandoned the *Examiner* in the wake of its condemnation by the bishop. In the initial stages of the dispute it gave preference to the anti-Parnellite side in its coverage, until its role as an alternative voice to the *Examiner* became largely redundant on the foundation of the *Westmeath Nationalist* in April 1891.[10] In contrast to the reticence of the *Westmeath Guardian*, the more overtly unionist *Athlone Times* was more inclined to speak its mind and was highly critical of what it called Parnell's 'disgusting outrage'. It was critical of his party also for largely ignoring the moral aspect of the controversy in the debates on Parnell's leadership.[11]

Nevertheless, in those days before opinion polls, it was difficult to gauge the public mood and both sides eagerly awaited the North Kilkenny by-election, which was the first real test on a national scale of the relative strengths of the opposing sides. Despite the advantages enjoyed by the Parnellites, the election in which Parnell himself campaigned strenuously led to a resounding defeat for his candidate by a margin of nearly two to one. Undeterred by this setback, Parnell was determined to press on and embarked on what Callanan called his 'railway odyssey', travelling over and back from his home in England each weekend to address meetings in Ireland – something that he had not done for several years.[12] Some of these journeys took him through Westmeath, as the county at the time was traversed by the main railway line from Dublin to the west of Ireland. At the stations where his train stopped, Parnell was prevailed upon to say a few words of encouragement to his loyal followers. While these visits were undoubtedly useful in maintaining morale among his supporters, their real benefit lay in providing opportunities for the *Examiner* and other Parnellite newspapers to bolster the political campaign – often by giving the impression that Parnellite support was stronger than it really was. An example of how one such visit was exploited by Hayden and his followers occurred in January, when Parnellites, assembled at Mullingar station to greet their 'chief', came face to face with a group of their opponents who had gathered to meet Parnell's arch rival Tim Healy, who was due in the station at the same time to address a public meeting later in the town. Both the *Freeman's Journal* and the *Examiner* recounted with obvious satisfaction how Healy had a hostile reception from the Parnellites and was forced later to address his supporters behind locked doors, while Hayden and Downes addressed what the *Freeman* described as an 'immense crowd' in the street outside.[13] We cannot assume of course that all of the audience were there for purely political reasons. From experience elsewhere in the country, Parnellite demonstrations of this sort attracted a significant element of the poorer classes in the towns and this is likely to have been the case in Mullingar as well. Archbishop Croke of Cashel described them as 'cornerboys, blackguards of every hue, discontented labourers, lazy and drunken artisans, aspiring politicians, Fenians, and in a word, all irreligious and anticlerical scoundrels in the country'.[14] A more charitable explanation, perhaps, might be that these were people in the main without power or influence – or the vote in many cases – who had nothing to lose in supporting an anti-establishment movement, which if it did not bring any improvement in their plight, might at least bring an element of excitement into their dreary lives. A well-known figure with an aura of intrigue and scandal attaching to him, such as Parnell, could always draw a crowd, even if many of them knew or cared little for the policies he advocated. For example, on the same day as the Mullingar incident, a crowd of 200 or so meeting Parnell at Athlone station had grown steadily, Pied Piper style, by the time he reached his hotel, swollen by crowds attending the annual horse fair in the town.[15]

Apart from this fickle element in Parnellite support, several more organized groups of Parnellite supporters were active throughout the county as early as January, mostly under the banner of the Parnell Leadership committee, which had been launched in Dublin in the previous month. The national committee included J.P. Hayden from Mullingar and Thomas Chapman of the *Westmeath Independent* from Athlone, but significantly also, the Revd Christopher Mullen, parish priest of Moynalty in Co Meath, believed to be the only priest in the Meath diocese to publicly identify with the Parnellites.[16] In addition to the national committee, a Westmeath branch was established in Mullingar that included among its membership Hayden and his loyal band of followers from

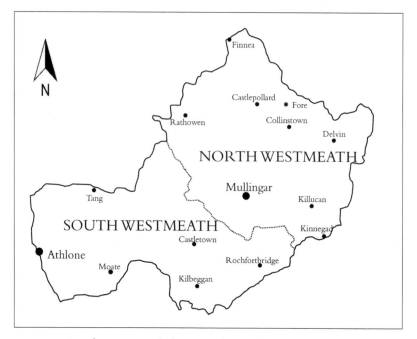

7. Map of Co. Westmeath showing parliamentary divisions (1885–1918)

the earlier waterworks dispute with the bishop.[17] In a short time, branches of the organization were set up also throughout the county in places such as Athlone, Kilbeggan, and Castlepollard. There was support also for the Parnellite cause from other nationalist organizations, among them the IRB (Irish Republican Brotherhood – sometimes known as the Fenians) and the GAA (Gaelic Athletic Association), although the latter organization despite its strong IRB links was, like the population in general, divided in its allegiance.[18]

The considerable advantages, both nationally and in Westmeath, that the Parnellite movement enjoyed in its early stages were not to last. Early in the new year their opponents, marshalling their forces for the battle ahead, founded a new organization, the Irish National Federation (INF), to counter the INL, which remained largely in the hands of the Parnellites. The new organization, with the clergy in the lead role as they had been in the INL previously, quickly established itself, growing from six branches in the county in the three months up to the end of March to a total of 11 branches by the end of June.[19] James Tuite, the local MP, was an early campaigner for the new organization, telling farmers and labourers in a speech in Mullingar that their success depended on it. At the same time, he denounced the Parnellite leaders in Mullingar as 'actuated more by a hatred of the bishops and priests than by love of Mr Parnell'.[20] Tuite was canvassing for the support of farmers and labourers, while also trying to ingratiate himself with the clergy who must have felt aggrieved that their old enemy Hayden had re-emerged to torment them. We know that Nulty in particular did feel aggrieved at the turn of events, describing Hayden as 'a man in Mullingar, who was well known … as an enemy of the Bishop, who was notorious all over Westmeath as his greatest enemy, and who was constantly vilifying and calumniating him'.[21] Nulty's anger was understandable in the circumstances, as Hayden had set himself up in opposition to clerical control of local politics and used the pages of the *Examiner* to support the Parnellite campaign in the county. It was clear that both the clergy and their anti-Parnellite colleagues needed a newspaper that would counter the influence of the *Examiner*. Now that the INF was up and running, this was their next priority.

This was the priority of their counterparts at a national level also and in March they brought out their own daily newspaper, the *National Press*, to challenge the *Freeman's Journal*. From the beginning, the *National Press*, in the absence of the party moderates Dillon and O'Brien in Galway gaol, upped the ante in the dispute and provided Tim Healy with a platform with which to mercilessly attack Parnell. The *National Press* was followed soon after by the launch of the *Westmeath Nationalist*, a weekly paper in the same stridently pro-clerical, anti-Parnellite vein as its national counterpart. The *Nationalist* was established by Jasper Tully, proprietor of the *Roscommon Herald*, assisted by his brother George. It had the backing of Nulty and his clergy and started with good intentions, proclaiming loftily 'we shall insult or attack no man because his opinions are not ours'.[22] It would, nevertheless, go on to do exactly the opposite and the intemperate nature of its attacks on its opponents, carried out in the name of religion and upholding the primacy of the Church, was remarkable even by the standards of the time. In contrast to the efforts made by the bishop and his clergy to destroy Hayden's paper, no attempt was made by them to rein in the *Nationalist*, although the scurrility of its language, ostensibly in their defence, can hardly have done anything to enhance the reputation of the Church among the population at large. The rivalry between the two nationalist newspaper proprietors in Mullingar and their political backers extended to the meeting rooms of the local poor law union who were quite unashamedly prepared to put their own political interests above those of the ratepayers they represented when they awarded the printing contract for the union to Hayden although Tully had submitted a lower tender.[23]

While the townspeople were divided in their allegiances, they were nonetheless more inclined to express their views publicly, in comparison to their more numerous country cousins, who were in the main more reticent. With more to lose, the farmers were less inclined to publicly express an opinion, particularly since it was unclear at the early stage of the dispute what the outcome would be. The evidence from the land struggle had shown that the farmers were prepared to become involved in politics when they could see a clear advantage accruing to themselves from such involvement. This time it was different. There was little to be gained from an internecine dispute that put at risk the goal of ownership of their farms and which also had the potential to poison relationships in close-knit interdependent rural communities. The farmers in the county, moreover, were not a homogenous community. Apart from differences in social status resulting from farm size, a high proportion were graziers often with considerable land holdings. This latter group attracted the ire of their small-farming counterparts, not least for the fact that many were town dwellers who enjoyed other sources of income as well as farming. For the small farmers who were more dependent on the goodwill of their neighbours for their livelihood, it was more difficult to take a stand. When the opportunity came in the 1892 general election to have their say, many did not vote at all, while those who did express a preference came down overwhelmingly on the majority side, forgetting, as Hayden recalled later, how Parnell had emancipated them from landlordism.[24]

In addition to their innate conservatism, the uncompromising anti-Parnellite stance of the clergy is likely to have been a significant factor also in shaping the views of the farming community. Woods has argued that in contrast to the towns, where there were a variety of educated men to provide leadership (this is confirmed in the case of Mullingar), in rural areas the priests had the field largely to themselves.[25] Apart from the close personal relationships between priests and people, the clergy possessed in the church pulpit an unparalleled platform with which to disseminate, not only the tenets of their faith, but also their anti-Parnellite views. Moreover, because generations of conditioning would have predisposed their congregations to accept whatever creed was preached from the pulpit, their words carried a weight that was infinitively greater than similar views expressed from a political platform or in the pages of a newspaper. Hayden himself ruefully acknowledged this clerical influence in the wake of the defeat of the Parnellite candidate in the 1892 election in South Westmeath, when he wrote in the *Examiner* that the rural dwellers of the constituency had 'voted for the priest'.[26]

The importance of clerical leadership was demonstrated also in the North Sligo by-election in early April when the Parnellite candidate polled a respectable 2,493 votes to the winner's 3,261 in a contest where priests were active not only on the anti-Parnellite side but on the Parnellite side as well. The priests' participation on the Parnellite side in the election was most likely influenced by the decision of one of the three local bishops, whose dioceses overlapped the constituency, to adopt a largely neutral stance in the dispute.[27] No such neutrality was exercised in the diocese of Meath, however, where Nulty imposed tight control on his priests, even to the extent of summoning dissident Revd Mullen of Moynalty to Mullingar to prevent him attending a Parnellite meeting in Navan on 1 March.[28] Despite his inflexible stance, Nulty was concerned at the effect the dispute was having on his flock, acknowledging to his congregation in Mullingar that 'he never knew on any occasion a division in which Irishmen had such feelings of antipathy towards one another'. Not wanting to exacerbate an already fraught situation, he adopted a conciliatory tone, remarking that 'there were business men, sensible men, and patriotic men, who loved their country, on both sides'. For good measure, he added that 'the Healyite party ... was a little intolerant too'.[29] Faced with open revolt in the eastern part of his diocese, his attitude soon changed. The same Dr Nulty could state in Navan just a few weeks later, that 'he did not see how anyone professing the Catholic religion could consistently with that religion support Mr Parnell'. Moreover, he refused to accept dues from councillors who opposed his nominees to the Navan poor law board.[30]

In Mullingar, however, the town commissioners were altogether a more amenable bunch. They registered their disapproval of a proposed visit by Parnell to the town for a public meeting in early May by proclaiming that it was 'insulting to our beloved, patriotic bishop'.[31] The meeting, intended by the Parnellites to be the showcase of their campaign in the county, and heavily promoted in the pages of the *Examiner*, did go ahead despite the opposition of the local clergy who waged a vigorous campaign against it. This included the reading at masses of a letter, on behalf of the bishop, discouraging the people from attending.[32] The efforts of the priests had their effect and when the day came, not even Parnell's fame or notoriety could entice the mass of the townspeople to come out to see him. Allowing for the fact that many of the disappointing turnout came from outside the district, the meeting could hardly have been described as a resounding success.[33] The *Nationalist* claimed that such was the level of opposition in the town to the visit, that no timber could be got locally for the platform or no conveyance could be procured in the town to transport Parnell from the station. In what was the ultimate indignity, no 'artisan' could be found to erect the platform, resulting in an 'ex-convict' having to do 'the dirty work' instead.[34] Indeed, the lack of enthusiasm in the town for the visit can be gauged from the fact that, contrary to the custom when Parnell visited a town, there were no green boughs to be seen on any of the houses. This was in marked contrast to his reception in Navan a couple of months earlier when evergreen arches spanned the streets and laurel boughs adorned the houses.[35] Nevertheless, in spite of what his detractors might say, support for Parnell was far from negligible. No less than 14 guardians from the Mullingar poor law union signed an address of welcome to him, as did the chairman, vice-chairman and deputy vice-chairman of the Athlone union. Responding to the addresses, Parnell, showing his awareness of the real power in the town, castigated his opponents as 'an oligarchy of pretenders and persons who arrogate to themselves superior wisdom to that possessed by the common herd with regard to political questions'. Hayden took up the same theme in his speech from the platform when he told the assembled crowd that 'they feared not persecution or the denunciations to which they were subjected Sunday after

Sunday'. While they 'respected their bishops and priests' and would defend their religion, 'this would never make them slaves to the preachers of that religion'. With an eye to the rural vote, Parnell concentrated on the farming community in his speech from the platform. He appealed to their self-interest with promises to exert pressure on the government in relation to the purchase of their holdings.[36] The irony of course was that the considerable influence he once commanded in the corridors of power had been greatly diminished by the split in the party, a situation that the conservative farmers of Westmeath would no doubt have understood.

The depths of the animosity between the two sides – or at least between the extreme Healyite faction of the party and the Parnellites – was laid bare for all to see just a few weeks after the Mullingar rally when the *National Press* published a series of articles accusing Parnell of misappropriating party funds entrusted to his care and provocatively inviting him to sue the newspaper for libel.[37] Parnell's failure to respond adequately to the challenge damaged his credibility at a crucial time when his support was already declining. He suffered a further series of hammer blows over the summer with the defection of the *Freeman's Journal* to his opponents and the resounding defeat for his candidate A.J. Kettle in the Carlow by-election. The bishops added to the mounting pressure when, on the day of his marriage to Katharine, they delivered a further stinging rebuke to his claims to the leadership of the party, stating in uncompromising terms, 'that Mr Parnell, by his public misconduct, has utterly disqualified himself to be their political leader … we therefore feel bound on this occasion to call on our people to repudiate his leadership'.[38] In Westmeath his support was ebbing too. Even the *Nationalist* could not have been accused of exaggerating when it exulted that 'the unholy cause of Parnellism is steadily on the wane.'[39] It could not resist the opportunity presented by Parnell's marriage, nevertheless, to pour renewed scorn on the deposed leader, sanctimoniously declaring:

> Oh, for the shame of the so-called 'marriage' of Parnell and the cast-off *mistress* of Capt. O'Shea! … Who would have ever dreamed that our country should be asked to drain such a cup of poison, and wallow in such unspeakable degradation? Thank God, the brainless, besotted followers, content to accept this servitude, are dwindling into insignificance.[40]

In contrast to its rival, the *Examiner's* response to the setbacks was to take refuge in the moral high ground, proclaiming, that

> A reverse here or a reverse there should not daunt us … nor considerations of mere success or failure should wholly influence us. There is something higher and holier than success. To act rightly according to the best of a person's belief and judgement, no matter whether the action may obtain popular approval, is what men should do.

Even though it could declare that 'There is no reason for being down-hearted or afraid of the future', it was clear that Parnellites in the county, no matter how honourable their cause, were indeed disheartened, faced with the magnitude of the task that confronted them. That task was made all the harder now that the *Nationalist* had entered the propaganda war.[41] To compound their problems, the struggle of the Parnellites to get their message across at public meetings was also becoming harder. A meeting in Castlepollard in June 1891, presided over by a local doctor and addressed by prominent Parnellite MPs, Tim Harrington and John Redmond, was, like the Mullingar rally, undermined by the action of the local priests who denounced it from the pulpit. One priest, quoted in the *Freeman's Journal*, warned that 'anyone who would attend, even out of curiosity, would have neither luck nor grace'.[42] The *Examiner* could not be controlled as easily, however, and continued to enjoy the backing of influential supporters on public bodies. The latest of these was the landlord-dominated county grand jury who, in a clear show of political partisanship, awarded its advertising contract to the *Examiner* and the *Guardian*, despite the *Nationalist*'s claim for equal treatment.[43] Still, apart from the political turmoil and perhaps because of it, the county was in an exceptionally peaceful and law-abiding state, so much so that 80 officers from the local constabulary, including 20 from Mullingar, could be sent north that year to police the annual twelfth of July celebrations.[44]

At the end of July, Dillon and O'Brien were released from Galway gaol, where they had been imprisoned since earlier in the year. By reaffirming their break with Parnell they removed any lingering hopes that the Parnellites might have entertained of gaining their support. On the evening of their release they were met by a large assembly when their train stopped at Mullingar station on its way to Dublin. Unlike Healy, Dillon and O'Brien were still held in respect by the Parnellites and Hayden and a few supporters were among the welcoming crowd, though greatly outnumbered by a mass of anti-Parnellites, including six priests.[45]

The failure of Dillon and O'Brien to support the Parnellites, or at least to offer an olive branch to their opponents was effectively the body blow that put paid to any lingering hopes of a revival in their fortunes. While support for the Parnellites in Westmeath, as measured by the numbers of INL branches, had remained constant up to the middle of the year, it declined precipitously after that, in contrast to the situation in neighbouring Meath where the INL continued to hold their ground for much longer.[46] Parnell himself was getting weaker and he seemed to sense that his struggle was coming to an end. Speaking in Listowel, Co. Kerry, in September 1891, he told the crowd, that if he was 'dead and gone tomorrow, the men who are fighting against English influence in Irish public life would fight on still; they would still be independent nationalists; they would still believe in the future of Ireland a nation'.[47] The end did come, unexpectedly, just a few weeks later when he died in the arms of his wife, thus ending a career marked by great achievement and, in the end, spectacular failure.

His funeral to Glasnevin cemetery, attended by upwards of 100,000 people, was itself a microcosm of Parnellite support. According to a Dublin Castle official 'there were few if any farmers present. Townspeople and labourers – and Fenians – composed the multitude'. 'Not a single priest was to be seen.'[48] Hayden, who brought out a special edition of the *Examiner* with black-bordered columns to mark Parnell's death, denounced in emotional terms the ingratitude of those, particularly the tenant farmers, who had benefited from the land reforms that Parnell did so much to bring about. He claimed that over 100 mourners travelled from Mullingar to the funeral and Hayden himself (reported in the *Freeman's Journal*) was among a select group of Parnellites who received the coffin of their dead chief on the pier at Kingstown (now Dun Laoghaire) when it arrived from England.[49] In addition to the *Examiner*, the *Westmeath Independent* and the *Athlone Times* also highlighted the ingratitude of the tenant farmers, while the *Guardian*'s coverage was characteristically non-committal and confined to two short factual reports of the death and funeral. The *Nationalist* on the other hand ignored the event altogether.[50] The *Freeman's Journal*, although by this time in the anti-Parnellite camp, was mindful of the dead leader's contribution to the national cause. It described him in a leading article on the day after the funeral as 'the foremost Irishman of the day' and expressed the hope that 'no man [would] attempt to carry bitterness or hostility beyond the grave'.[51] It was a forlorn hope, however, and the struggle for supremacy between the warring parties continued undiminished and if anything with added intensity, reinforced by the sense of grievance on the part of the Parnellites that their leader had been driven to his grave by the virulence of the campaign waged against him.[52]

3. The verdict of the people

The months following Parnell's death saw the opposing sides mobilizing their forces for the general election that was expected in the following year. Both sides looked forward to the election, but with different expectations. The Parnellites hoped that the election might mark a change in their fortunes while their opponents expected that it would deliver the killer blow that would finally mark the end of Parnellism. In the meantime, the rivalry in local politics continued. Hayden and Kerrigan stood again in October for the Mullingar town commissioners but, with the strength of the clerical opposition ranged against them, it was hardly surprising that they were again defeated. More significantly, though, they retained much the same share of the vote as they had in previous elections, indicating that while the Parnellite campaign was increasingly running out of steam, it still retained, in Mullingar at least, the backing of the same sizable minority as it had before.[1] The size of the vote, moreover, represented a continuing reproach to the bishop and his clergy and a denial of their assumed right to decide who should represent the ratepayers on the town commissioners.

How much this vote was support for the Parnellite cause and how much it was a protest vote, as Hayden claimed, for 'the liberty of each man in the community to think and act for himself on all matters affecting the town or the country', is impossible to gauge, although to a large extent at this time, the idea of political independence and Parnellism were synonymous.[2] It is reasonable to assume that some at least of the vote was Protestant, as the town contained a large Protestant population; a community that the *Westmeath Nationalist* could assert – under the guise of Tory – voted en-masse for Hayden and Kerrigan.[3] While the existence of Protestant/unionist support for the Parnellites is confirmed by the co-operation between the two groups on the Mullingar poor law board and by the support for the *Westmeath Examiner* from the Westmeath grand jury, the motivation for this support is less clear. Possible reasons may have been a desire on the part of unionists to curtail the political power of the Catholic Church while at the same time weakening the nationalist movement for home rule. A home rule Ireland, in which unionists would be greatly outnumbered, was anathema to most Protestants, including those in Westmeath. This is evident from the scathing report in the *Athlone Times* of the by-election in Cork city which was fought out between the two nationalist factions for the parliamentary seat left vacant by the death of Parnell. With withering sarcasm, the paper recounted how the Celt, in all his war paint ... exhibits the real raw material on which sensible Saxons are asked to build up home rule or self government. What an idea! These brawling, fighting factions to guide the destinies of Ireland! Gilbert could not imagine anything half so ridiculous or grotesquely absurd.[4]

By this yardstick, the Protestant support for Hayden and Kerrigan could hardly be construed as a ringing endorsement of Parnellism or its principles; more a case of the lesser of two evils. Regardless of the motivation of the Protestant vote, it is unlikely that the Parnellite tally in the town was swelled by many working-class or artisan voters. The numbers of voters in these categories would have been small in any case, given the property qualification for the franchise. Both labour organizations in the town were firmly within the clerical sphere of influence, with a local priest serving as honorary president of the Mullingar workingmen's club, while the recently established Mullingar trade and labour union had clearly indicated which side it was on when it sought and obtained the bishop's approval for its first programme.[5] The franchise qualifications on the other hand would have favoured the business community and it is likely that a share of the business vote, both Protestant and Catholic, went to the Parnellites, if the volume of commercial advertising carried in the town's two nationalist newspapers can be taken as a guide. Although there was little duplication in commercial advertising between the two papers, a sign in itself of the polarization on politico/religious lines of the business community, the *Examiner* attracted at least as much of this advertising as its rival – a situation that continued even after the *Nationalist* was well established.

In mobilizing support, the *Examiner* was an important weapon in the armoury of the Parnellites. In a tribute to its continuing influence, despite the advent of the *Nationalist*, it continued to be a target of the clergy, with Dr Langan, an Athlone priest, calling on delegates at an INF convention in Mullingar to 'wipe' it out.[6] Their attempts to silence the paper, however, often only served to provide propaganda coups for Hayden and his followers. For example, at a public meeting of ratepayers in Mullingar in December, the reporter from the *Examiner* was ordered out of the hall by the Revd Thomas Drum, the administrator of the parish, on the basis that the hall belonged to the Church, allowing Hayden as a ratepayer to take his place and publicly challenge the priest's right to curtail press freedom at a public meeting. This was good ground to make a stand on and predictably Hayden made much of the incident in the pages of the *Examiner*, telling his readers:

> The course adopted by Father Drum and the statements which he made are curiously suggestive of what the country would be reduced if there was not in it that strong party of independence which is fighting so manfully for the right of every Irishman to freedom of thought,

expression and action. He has given them a justification for their policy and shown the great necessity which exists for a strong and active party to assert that freedom which is so much required and without which legislative freedom would be of little value.[7]

This and other actions directed against the *Examiner* by the clergy not only provided political ammunition for Hayden; it provided good copy for his newspaper also, and may – as he himself claimed – even have increased its circulation.[8] Nevertheless, it cannot have been an easy time for the *Examiner*, faced with cut-throat competition from its new rival and the best efforts of Nulty and his priests to destroy it. But, survive it did, against all the odds. This can be attributed, in part, to a sizable and influential minority who were prepared to support the paper with its advertising. However, it has to be acknowledged that at least some of the public advertising and printing contracts that it received were awarded with a degree of political bias, a point which arch-rival Jasper Tully never ceased to make. Equally important to its survival was the existence of a substantial readership prepared to ignore the views of the bishop when it came to their choice of paper. The size of this readership was reflected in the circulation of the *Examiner*, which was still – by the standards of the time – a healthy 600 in 1892. While no circulation figures survive for the *Westmeath Nationalist*; James Tuite MP could claim, not long after the paper was established, that its circulation was 2,500. This figure seems exaggerated, though, considering that its sister-paper, the long-established *Roscommon Herald*, had a circulation of just 773 at the time.[9]

The general election campaign in the county kicked off in earnest early in the new year with the INF holding a county convention in Mullingar. The convention brought together delegates from all over the county and was attended by more than 20 priests. Delegates heard speeches from James Tuite and also from Tim Healy whose intemperate language since the split began did much to prolong the bitterness between the two sides. In a letter read to the convention, Nulty threw his weight behind the campaign, offering the services of his priests to actively assist in the formation of local branches of the organization. He went on to describe the Parnellite opposition in forthright terms as 'a political organization that is manifestly incapable of accomplishing the smallest amount of good, and … contains in itself the elements of its own disillusion'. He continued: 'Possibly … at the coming general election it may make a last desperate and expiring effort to ruin the national cause, to prolong the country's agony'. Despite his belief that Parnellism was on its knees, he retained a healthy respect for its fighting prowess, remarking that 'the country cannot be too often warned or too well prepared to resist the deadly and insidious onslaught that Parnellism may then make on it'.[10] While it was clear that Parnellism and its extermination was an obsession for the bishop, his sense of urgency did not filter down to the ordinary people. Although it was a market day in the town and large numbers were on the streets, the delegates and MPs were ignored on their way to and from the hall in which the convention was held.[11] While the general public may have grown weary of a dispute played out by the churchmen and the political class, largely without their participation, it did have its effects on the most vulnerable. An incident that occurred in Mullingar in the early part of 1892 illustrates this. Notices posted throughout the town, most likely organized by Hayden and his supporters, claimed that collections taken up at church gates and intended for the relief of evicted tenants were being used for the support of the INF. Subscribers were warned also that they were 'approving of the ... defamers and murderers of Parnell'. Whatever about the veracity of the claim of diverting funds, the protest did affect the size of the collection, demonstrating how in an increasingly fractious dispute the welfare of vulnerable tenants was sacrificed in the pursuit of narrow sectional interests.[12] Even if the general public showed little interest in the political infighting, the clergy's active and partisan involvement in the dispute and the continuing unrelenting campaign by the *Examiner* against them was taking its toll on the traditional loyalty of the people towards their priests. Nulty himself acknowledged this situation, when he told his congregation in Mullingar around this time that 'there was a coldness between the priests and the people'.[13]

His concern did not mean that there was any let up in his struggle against the Parnellites, and Nulty saw the threat of Parnellism everywhere, even in the non-political election for the salaried post of county coroner. The election to fill this position was called in January 1892, following the untimely death of Dr Kerrigan, one of Hayden's most faithful comrades-in-arms. Nulty had magnanimously chosen not to oppose Kerrigan when he stood for the position five years previously, even though he was already at that stage one of the Hayden 'clique' who opposed his waterworks scheme. This time he was in a less forgiving mood and made clear his opposition to candidates for the post who were in any way associated with his opponents. One such candidate was the late coroner's brother, who, although he had a much lower public profile, was, nevertheless, suspected by the bishop of having the same political views. In an address at Sunday mass in Mullingar – which Hayden, in his account in the *Examiner* provocatively headed 'No Protestant nor Parnellite need apply' – Nulty urged his congregation not to vote for either a Conservative or Parnellite as coroner, as 'the Conservatives of the county always retained any office of emolument for their own followers whenever they have the power, as they do in Belfast and elsewhere', while 'the Parnellites were anti-Catholic ... [and] were always ready to oppose anything a bishop or a priest undertook'. His remarks did not bode well for equal treatment of minorities in any future Catholic majority government, a point that was not lost on Hayden, who could proclaim in the *Examiner* that the bishop's statement was 'not calculated to reconcile the Protestant minority in the country to home rule'.[14] But neither side emerged from the affair with much credit. The election for coroner, which should have been conducted on the basis of suitability for the post, regardless of political allegiance or religious affiliation, had become yet another battleground in the ongoing struggle for supremacy between the two warring factions. On the day, however, the electorate proved less willing to play the political game and voted largely for candidates with whom they were familiar in their local areas. Nevertheless, the bishop's man, John Gaynor, a solicitor from Athlone and prominent INF member, was the winner, but despite Nulty's advice the late coroner's brother came in second of the four candidates who stood, with the *Nationalist* grudgingly conceding that he had received 'whatever Parnellite support was going'.[15]

The spirited showing of Kerrigan in the election for coroner could not hide the continuing decline in Parnellite support throughout the county. By this time, the INL was in terminal decline although it continued to enjoy support in the neighbouring county of Meath.[16] The extent of the decline was reflected in the Parnellites' poor performance in the election for poor law guardians held in March, where they lost seven seats in the county, all of which fell to their opponents.[17] Still, they clung to the hope that the upcoming general election would lead to a change in their fortunes and galvanize a latent support that they hoped still existed. Despite the presence of Hayden and his followers in the northern parliamentary division, it was clear as the election approached and selection conventions got under way that the south was the better organized of the two constituencies in the county and carried the best prospects for success. The Parnellites in the southern division got off to a bad start, however, when they selected a Catholic landlord, Charles O'Donoghue, who, lacking the aura of a Parnell, was hardly calculated to appeal to the predominantly small farming electorate. They may have had little choice; as Murray speculates, O'Donoghue's ability to pay his election expenses may have been a factor in his nomination.[18] While his status as a landlord may not have enhanced his standing with the nationalist electorate, it was an advantage as far as the *Athlone Times* was concerned. Opting for O'Donoghue over the outgoing MP, Donal Sullivan, it declared in its usual fashion: 'we much prefer him, an extensive local resident landlord, to the political ninny who now represents the division in Parliament, and who seems to have had just brains enough to desert … from the principles and party he was elected to support.' At the same time, it did not believe O'Donoghue would win because of the influence of the clergy.[19] Although it was hardly a very auspicious start to their campaign, there was still considerable support for the Parnellites across the constituency, with a number of public meetings attracting large crowds, including one at Castletown that was attended by more than 3,000 people.[20] Regardless of their choice of candidate, the Parnellites faced an uphill battle to unseat Donal Sullivan, who was selected again at a convention in Mullingar where his parliamentary colleague James Tuite was also chosen to contest the North Westmeath constituency. Both candidates were proposed by priests: Dr Langan of Athlone proposed Sullivan and the Revd Curry of Collinstown proposed Tuite.[21]

Although Hayden could confidently claim in the *Examiner*, referring to the southern division, that one of the two seats 'is already practically conceded to the Independent party', he could not, even with his considerable rhetorical skills, make any similar claims for the northern division.[22] There, it was apparent, the Parnellites were in disarray. When they managed to find a candidate – Alexander Blane, a sitting MP who represented South Armagh – they struggled to come up with the deposit of £200 to secure his nomination.[23] In a collection held in Mullingar to defray the election expenses, the *Freeman's Journal* claimed that the Parnellites could not raise enough money to pay their candidate's third-class train fare from Armagh.[24] If that was not enough, Blane had the added disadvantage of being unknown in the division, in contrast to his opponent James Tuite, who unlike many nationalist MPs at the time was a native of the constituency that he represented.

Notwithstanding the advantages their candidates enjoyed, the considerable weight of the clergy was thrown behind both anti-Parnellites, even to the extent of permitting an election rally for Tuite to be held in the local church in Collinstown, when rain disrupted the planned outdoor event.[25] While the chances of his candidates being returned were good, in the Westmeath part of his diocese at least, Nulty was not taking any chances. In an unprecedented intervention, he exhorted his parishioners in a pastoral read at masses throughout his diocese on the Sunday before the election not to vote for Parnellite candidates, saying that 'no intelligent, or well-informed man can continue and remain a Catholic, as long as he elects to cling to Parnellism'.[26] While it is impossible to quantify the effect his intervention had, it cannot but have been significant, prompting the two unsuccessful Parnellite candidates in the Meath part of his diocese, who were both narrowly defeated, to lodge petitions to unseat the successful candidates on the grounds of clerical interference in the election.

In Westmeath, in contrast, the results were not in doubt, with the anti-Parnellites running out decisive winners. O'Donoghue polled 30 per cent of the vote in South Westmeath, due mainly to the support of townsmen in Athlone and Kilbeggan and the better-organized campaign conducted on his behalf. However, in the northern division, the contest was over before it began. Even the *Examiner* was forced to concede that the candidate Blane was only in the constituency 'for a few hours' on his nomination day, and that on his behalf no canvass had been made or meetings held. Not surprisingly, he polled just 11 per cent of the vote, many of these from the town of Mullingar, which accounted for almost half the Parnellite vote (Table 1).[27] The priests, meanwhile, who had 'left no stone unturned' in support of their candidates,[28] came in for particular criticism for the part they played in the election from the Parnellite newspapers in the county. The *Examiner* claimed that 'intimidation of the worst sort was used on and off the altar, and it is little wonder indeed that it succeeded in its object'. It gave the example of South Westmeath where 'outside the booths in almost every instance numbers of priests were stationed canvassing the electors and from several districts they marched their parishioners to the voting places in solid masses to cast their votes'. It was the same in the northern constituency, the *Examiner* went on. There 'the booths were all well manned with priests inside and outside, and everything in the way of argument, entreaty and threat was used to induce the voters to poll for the Whig [anti-Parnellite]'.[29] The *Westmeath Independent*, which headed its report of the election result 'a clerical victory', claimed 'the clerical party has triumphed in South Westmeath. Intimidation – threats of punishment, temporal and eternal – have achieved a victory that argument or reason could never accomplish.'[30]

Table 1. General election results in Westmeath and Meath, 1892

Constituency	*Anti-Parnellite*		*Parnellite*		*Anti-P. %*
North Westmeath	J. Tuite	2,878	A. Blane	379	88.36%
South Westmeath	D. Sullivan	2,535	C. O'Donoghue	1,080	70.12%
North Meath	M. Davitt	2,549	P. Mahony	2,146	54.29%
South Meath	P. Fulham	2,212	J.J. Dalton	2,199	50.14%

(Source: Brian Walker, *Parliamentary election results in Ireland, 1801–1922* (Dublin, 1978)).

While clerical influence and the bishop's pastoral were undoubtedly key factors in the success of the anti-Parnellite candidates, it was hardly the full story as the close result of the election in Meath showed. In the two constituencies of that county, Parnellite candidates narrowly lost. One, a relative unknown (like Blane), came within 22 votes of victory in the northern division, while outgoing MP Pierce Mahony also lost out by a small margin to former Land League leader Michael Davitt in the southern division (Table 1).[31] In South Roscommon, the Parnellites actually emerged victorious with Luke Hayden (brother of John) polling more than 60 per cent of the votes cast, while his counterpart in North Roscommon was just 49 votes behind the anti-Parnellite candidate. While these results were the exception rather than the rule as far as the Parnellites were concerned, they showed that with effective leadership and strong local organizations they could hold their own against the power and influence of the Catholic Church. In Westmeath, in contrast, the anti-Parnellites held all the trump cards. They benefited from strong candidates, in the outgoing MPs Tuite and Sullivan, who actively canvassed throughout the county in the months before the election.[32] More importantly, their support organization the INF, with the backing of the clergy, was more active than its Parnellite counterpart the INL which, in the view of Captain Stokes of the RIC, was 'practically extinct'.[33] This is reflected in public contributions to the election expenses of the candidates in Westmeath, with the anti-Parnellites collecting three times as much as their opponents, whereas in Meath the situation was reversed, with donations to the Parnellites double those of their opponents.[34] Clerical leadership and influence had proportionally a greater effect on the election outcome in Westmeath than in either Meath or Roscommon. This was due to the relative weakness of the Parnellite organization, who, particularly in North Westmeath – and despite the presence of Hayden and his supporters – proved incapable of mounting an effective challenge to their opponent's superiority in manpower and resources. This was particularly so in rural parts of the county where the police reported that the Parnellites lacked the 'local agents' to bring supporters to the polling stations. In contrast, the anti-Parnellites benefited enormously from the active support of the Catholic clergy, not just in their direct role in getting out the anti-Parnellite vote, but also in their indirect role in discouraging Parnellite voters from coming out to vote, and police reports back up the Parnellite view that the majority of abstentions were of Parnellite supporters unwilling to 'incur the odium' of opposing their local clergy.[35]

Understandingly, therefore, the priests were jubilant at the extent of their victory, even triumphalist, if the reaction of one of their number, Revd O'Reilly, can be considered typical. Addressing the crowd from James Tuite's house in Mullingar, after the result in North Westmeath had been declared, O'Reilly called for Cork to be the location of a future home rule parliament, instead of Dublin. He suggested also that traders boycott Dublin goods, to bring Dubliners who voted overwhelmingly for Parnellite candidates in the election to what he called 'a sense of their duty'.[36] Nulty's return to Mullingar a couple of weeks later, after a visitation of part of his diocese, was the occasion of another display of triumphalism by the clergy, when the bishop was welcomed back to the town in what the *Examiner* sarcastically called a 'spontaneous' demonstration by the people, but which it claimed was organized by the clergy. At the demonstration, addresses were read to the bishop from local bodies, including the Mullingar town commissioners and INF, congratulating him 'on the victories gained in his diocese over Toryism, factionism, and blackguardism combined'. Not surprisingly, the two sides could not agree on the size of the crowd at the event. According to the *Examiner*, it 'was not very large', while the clericalist *Drogheda Independent* reported that 'five thousand people thronged the streets and filled the air with salvos of cheering'.[37]

The jubilation of the clergy rings hollow, however, when one considers that the object of the anti-Parnellites and particularly the Church since Parnell's death had been to exterminate Parnellism and all it stood for. This they had singularly failed to do, and while the margin of victory in the election in Westmeath had been decisive, it was much less so in Meath. In both parts of the diocese, the bishop's assumed right to dictate to the people who would represent them on public boards and in parliament had been challenged as never before by a revitalized Catholic middle class and moreover his authority had been undermined, with his pronouncements criticized and his priests publicly ridiculed. In addition the Church itself had alienated a sizable minority of the Catholic community by its actions. The remaining years of Nulty's life would see him attempting to justify his role in the dispute and to repair the damage that had been done both to his own reputation and that of the Church in his diocese, although there is no evidence that he harboured any regrets for the prominent and controversial role that he played in the dispute.

4. The aftermath

Parnellism remained vibrant in some parts of the country following the 1892 general election but in Westmeath it was a spent force. The poor electoral result in the county left not even a glimmer of hope of a comeback. Even the inveterate campaigner Hayden bowed to the inevitable and for the first time in many years he did not contest the election for the Mullingar town commissioners held in October 1892. By the time the next election came around the following year the electors had lost interest too, with only 67 voting out of an electorate of 237. This was in sharp contrast to the heady days of the late 1880s and early 1890s when close to 200 turned out to vote.[1] In a further indication of the poor prospects for Parnellism in the county following the general election, the Mullingar poor law guardians awarded their printing contract to the *Westmeath Nationalist*; victory at last for what Tully, in his characteristic style, labelled 'all the forces hostile to our faith and country'.[2] The next general election, when it came in 1895, served only to confirm the rout of Parnellism in the county, with the two sitting MPs, Tuite and Sullivan, returned unopposed in a contest that saw 71 anti-Parnellites elected nationally in contrast to just 9 of their opponents. While the defeat of Parnellism was complete in Westmeath it had a much slower decline in Meath. There, despite their loss by narrow margins of the two by-elections caused by the successful outcome of the petitions to unseat the winning candidates in the 1892 election, the Parnellites staged a comeback in 1895 with the election in South Meath of John Howard Parnell, a brother of the dead leader.

Why there should be such a variation in the level of Parnellite support between the two counties is an intriguing question, considering that the bishop was actively involved in the anti-Parnellite campaign in both parts of his diocese. There were obvious differences in the quality of the Parnellite leadership in Meath and the strength of its organization compared with those of Westmeath but these alone do not explain why Parnellism had such widespread appeal in Meath compared with its neighbour. A comparison of the two counties in terms of age profile, religious composition, levels of prosperity, urban/rural ratio and literacy levels does not provide any obvious explanation either (Table 2). There were no significant differences between the two counties, for example, in the numbers of males between the ages of 15 and 39 in the population, a cohort in which those with more radical leanings might be expected to be concentrated. Nor was there any difference between the proportions of Protestants and Catholics in both counties, which might indicate a Parnellite advantage for the county with the greater number of Protestants. There were differences, however, in the numbers of the population living on agricultural holdings over £15 in valuation, with significantly greater numbers in this category in Meath than in Westmeath (48% as against 39%). This variation could be expected to favour the Parnellites in Meath, as Parnellite support – outside of the towns where the Parnellite vote was heavily concentrated – tended to come disproportionately from larger farmers. Yet this advantage could be said to be counterbalanced by the greater numbers of Westmeath's inhabitants living in towns in the election year (27% in Westmeath, 22% in Meath). Literacy rates provide no clues either as these were the same in both counties. Lawlor cites the fact that Parnell was a former representative for Meath as a factor in the level of Parnellite support there, while Murray writes that Westmeath's inhabitants 'were prepared to accept clerical dictation' even before the 1892 election defeat, a view given some weight by the majority support for the bishop in his battle with the Mullingar 'clique' and the *Westmeath Examiner*.[3] The fact that the bishop lived in Mullingar and could adopt a more direct approach to his opponents, at a formative stage, may also have been significant in this regard. In addition, the Church had the support from early on of the two Westmeath MPs, in contrast to the situation in Meath where both MPs took the Parnellite side following the split, although one of the two did not stand in the subsequent election.

Table 2. Statistical comparison, Westmeath and Meath, 1891

	Westmeath	Meath
Males aged between 15 and 39 years of age as percentage of total male population.	39%	38%
Roman Catholic proportion of population.	92%	93%
Percentage of population living on agricultural holdings over £15 valuation.	39%	48%
Proportion of population non-resident on agricultural holdings.	27%	22%
Percentage of population 5 years of age and over who can neither read nor write.	16%	16%

(Sources: *Census of Ireland, 1891, Part I: Volume I*; Ibid., *Part II, General Report*).

While the reasons for the differences in support for the Parnellites between the two counties are inconclusive, there is no disputing that the bishop had won the war in his diocese – more convincingly in Westmeath than in Meath – but at a price. His conduct in the campaign had brought down on his head a torrent of criticism, not just in Ireland but in Britain as well, where Tory and unionist critics cited Nulty's interference in the 1892 election as grounds for their opposition to the second home rule bill introduced by the Liberal government in 1893.[4] His treatment of the *Examiner* drew much criticism and especially his renewed condemnation of the paper made in early 1894 which, unlike the previous censure, clearly indicated that any 'man' who read the *Examiner* was guilty of sin, thus earning the paper the nickname, 'the mortal sin', by which it was popularly known for years afterwards.[5] This renewed and more serious threat to his paper forced Hayden once again to appeal, in the first instance, to Cardinal Logue in Armagh (appointed cardinal in 1893) and finally, to the Prefect of Propaganda Fide in Rome. In his appeal, Hayden maintained that Nulty's proscription of the *Examiner* had been intended to ruin his business and had its origins in Hayden's objection to the bishop's waterworks scheme some years before.[6] The Vatican, in its investigation of the matter, disregarded Hayden's plea and concurred with the action taken by Nulty. The first Hayden heard of the judgment was when the decision was read from the altar in Mullingar several months after he made his appeal, prompting him to complain indignantly to Logue that his appeal was treated with contempt and that he had received neither a reply nor acknowledgment from the Church authorities.[7] There is no record of a reply to his letter on this occasion either. However, the affair did have a silver lining, as far as Hayden was concerned, allowing him to exploit to the full in the *Examiner* his harsh treatment at the hands of the Church. Adding to the pressure on Nulty, the matter was reported by other publications, among them *The Times* and the *Irish Daily Independent* – with the *Irish Daily Independent* printing copies of the correspondence between Hayden and the Church authorities.[8] The bishop's treatment of the *Examiner* even became an election issue in an English parliamentary constituency where it was portrayed by unionists as an example of how property rights would be infringed under home rule. Responding to his English critics on that occasion, Nulty denied that his objection to the paper was due to Hayden's objection to his waterworks scheme. It was, he maintained, based on the *Examiner*'s 'persistent abuse of the priests', which 'tended largely to undermine their influence and to lower them in the estimation of those who were bound to respect them'.[9] It was clear from his reply that the bishop and his clergy expected to shelter behind the wall of deference that traditionally separated them from the laity, while they themselves enjoyed the freedom to speak their minds, often in very intemperate language. This is indicated by the bishop's contemptuous dismissal of his opponents in Mullingar at the time of the waterworks controversy in 1888 and by the ongoing abuse of Hayden in the *Nationalist*.[10] The scandalous effect on the Catholic population of Hayden's disobedience is clearly what troubled the bishop. Thus, Hayden's objection to Nulty's waterworks scheme and in particular Hayden's publication of the ensuing controversy in the *Examiner*, were the most likely reasons why he condemned the paper in 1888. His later more extreme action towards the newspaper, although undoubtedly influenced by the acrimony generated by the Parnell split, was at heart a reaction to Hayden's continuing refusal to submit to his authority and a reflection also of his personal antipathy towards the *Examiner* for its continuing role in undermining that authority.

But perhaps the most serious criticism that was levelled against the bishop was in respect of his pastoral letter issued in advance of the general election of 1892, where he threatened Parnellites with expulsion from the Church if they did not mend their ways. In his pastoral Nulty described Parnellism, which he likened to paganism, as a 'great moral, social, and religious evil', which worked 'to break the golden link of love that has bound "the priests and the people"'. Even though Parnell was dead, there was no attempt made by the bishop in his pastoral or in the pamphlet which he published subsequently, defending it, to distinguish between the 'crime' of Parnell and the motivations of those who had supported him. Instead, Parnellites were condemned by association, for what Nulty, quoting the Irish bishops, called, the movement's 'false, vicious, and corrupt morals'.[11] The incongruity of Nulty's position was recognized even by the anti-Parnellite candidate in the South Meath election, Michael Davitt, when he stated that 'the mistake made by Dr Nulty in his pastoral, and by the priests in their interpretation of its contents ... was to treat Parnellites as if they had committed Parnell's sin'.[12] It was unlikely that many Parnellites did in fact condone Parnell's 'sin', and most, including Hayden, were at pains to express their loyalty to the Church in religious matters. It was different, though, when it came to what they saw as political issues, where they reserved the right to exercise their own judgment and to act accordingly. It was this defiance of his authority that was at the root of Nulty's condemnation of the Parnellites and which resulted in his unprecedented intervention in the election and his threat to expel them from the Church. The example of Nulty's autocratic response to the challenge posed to his authority by Hayden and his followers, which occurred long before Parnell's moral lapse became an issue for him or the hierarchy, adds weight to this argument. It was clear from his pastoral that Nulty was very concerned with the effect that Parnellism, and specifically 'its newspapers and its orators' was having on the authority and reputation of the bishops and priests. He claimed that the priests, for reasons strikingly similar to those he advanced for his ban on the *Examiner* in 1888, were subjected to 'scorn and ridicule' and brought into 'contempt, odium, and unpopularity with their flocks'.[13] Although he maintained that his argument against Parnellism was essentially on religious grounds, his concerns with the effects of the rebellion of the laity are the same as when the issue was the purely secular one of the Mullingar waterworks scheme of the late 1880s, when he accused Hayden and his followers of being motivated by an 'unholy aversion, and dislike for their clergy', seeking to make them 'odious and unpopular' with their flocks.[14] Parnellism was a manifestation on a grand scale of the rebellion against his authority and that of his clergy of those days, to be resisted in the same uncompromising fashion, not least since his opponents then were now Parnellites. As the example of the Mullingar waterworks controversy and the subsequent Parnell crisis showed, the bishop was not prepared to brook criticism of himself or his clergy or to tolerate any challenge to their authority. Nulty's intervention in the election, therefore, was a reflection not only of his desire to stamp out Parnellism in the diocese for its continuing defiance of his authority and that of his clergy, but was at the same time a restatement of his 'divine' right to have his judgment on the Parnell crisis and the suitability of candidates for public office accepted by the laity without question or debate.[15]

Despite the criticism that rained down on him, Nulty remained unapologetic in relation to his treatment of the *Examiner* or of his intervention in the election and while his reputation abroad and in the eyes of many of his countrymen may have been tarnished, he still enjoyed the respect and affection of the vast majority of the county's inhabitants. This was demonstrated by a lavish banquet in his honour in Mullingar in late 1895 where he showed he had lost none of his appetite for politics. Making an impassioned call on that occasion for unity among the three warring factions into which the party had divided following the 1892 election, he described them in his usual outspoken manner as a 'disorganized mob, who have no influence or authority whatsoever'.[16] His wide-ranging condemnation did not mean that he had adopted a position of neutrality between the different factions, however, with the *Examiner* reporting that in the following year he had summoned a number of his parish priests to what it called an 'episcopal star chamber' to censure them for their Parnellite sympathies.[17] He was not done with the Mullingar waterworks either, entering the fray once again (at the age of 78) with a counter-proposal of his own in opposition to a new scheme drawn up by the poor lawboard.[18]

Despite his continuing interest in politics and in the public affairs of his town, his life was drawing inexorably to a close and so too was Hayden's period in the political wilderness. The bishop's death on Christmas Eve 1898 was the signal for the young newspaper editor (still only in his thirties) to re-emerge on the political stage. He would go on to play a major role in the politics of his adopted county in the years ahead. He was helped on his way by his status as an MP, having succeeded in the previous year to his brother's parliamentary seat in South Roscommon following the latter's untimely death. Following the re-unification of the IPP in 1900, under Parnellite John Redmond, he became president of the North Westmeath United Irish League (UIL) – the successor organization to the INL and the INF – remaining in that role until the effective demise of the IPP in 1918. His tenure at the helm of the UIL in North Westmeath was not without its controversy, being marred by bitter factional rivalry between his followers and those of Laurence Ginnell, an agrarian agitator and one-time Hayden ally, who became MP for North Westmeath in 1906. The controversy did not inhibit his own parliamentary career, however, and he was returned unopposed in each successive election in South Roscommon until his defeat by prominent republican Harry Boland in the Sinn Féin landslide of 1918. In a busy life, he served also on the Irish board of agriculture and was a 'close friend and confidant' of John Redmond.[19] All the while he continued at the helm of the *Examiner* and when he died in 1954 he was reputed to be the longest-serving newspaper editor in the country, having served for a record 72 years.

While Hayden's star was in the ascendant in the years after Nulty's death, that of the clergy was going in the opposite direction. Without Nulty's guiding hand and with the marginalization of the Healyite faction to which they had given their allegiance they had little choice but to accept a more subservient role in the reunited nationalist movement than they had hitherto enjoyed.[20] Nowhere was this more evident than in the North Westmeath UIL selection convention for the 1906 election when, with Hayden serving as chairman, and even with 18 priests as ex-officio delegates, the clergy's candidate, Sir Walter Nugent, was outvoted by Ginnell who at the time had the support of Hayden.[21] For Hayden, the clergy's diminished status in the nationalist movement and his own political rehabilitation was vindication at last, both for his policy of opposition to clerical domination of politics in the county and for the freedom for Catholics like himself to take an independent line in politics to that espoused by their Church.

Thus, while the Parnell split in Westmeath marked a victory for Nulty and his clergy in the short term, it represented a defeat in the medium term, in that the fragmentation of the party that the split brought about ultimately reduced their influence in the reunited nationalist movement and dealt a blow to their authority that would take time to heal. For Hayden, it was the opposite: humiliating defeat at the time of the split with its divisive outcome providing an opportunity – after a period in the political wilderness – to advance his political career. In addition, for the Catholic middle class he represented, it marked their coming of age as a political force independent of Church authority while for their clerical opponents it provided a harsh lesson in the limits of that authority.

While the political effects of the Parnell split were significant and far-reaching, it was the human cost of the controversy that lingered in the folk memory long after the political tumult had died away. This was the aspect of the dispute that was still on Hayden's mind some 60 years later when he recalled in his memoir: 'Our people were completely rent into two violently opposite parties. Old friendships were broken. In some instances families were divided. Language, of which many were afterwards ashamed, was freely used.' Hayden's description of the Parnell crisis as 'one of the saddest in the melancholy history of Ireland' indicates the lasting impression this bitter and acrimonious dispute had on one of the most prominent actors in the drama. It provides also a salutary epitaph for the Parnell split in Westmeath.[22]

Conclusion

This short book has argued that the Parnell split in Westmeath, while ostensibly about Parnell's suitability for the leadership of the IPP, was at the same time a struggle between a section of the Catholic middle class and the Church for the control of local politics in the county. It was in many ways an unequal struggle and the Parnellites in Westmeath found themselves greatly outnumbered and, in the end, decisively defeated by the might of the clerical and lay opposition directed against them. This was not the case, however, in the neighbouring county of Meath, where David Lawlor has shown that public support for the Parnellites was stronger and more enduring, even though both counties were situated within the diocese of Meath, whose bishop Dr Nulty took a prominent and divisive part in the dispute.

The crisis in Westmeath was marked by the rivalry between John P. Hayden, the leader of a group of young middle-class men in Mullingar and editor of the *Westmeath Examiner*, and Bishop Thomas Nulty; a rivalry that had begun before the split occurred, and continued after it had effectively ended. The origins of this rivalry in the years before the split are crucial to our understanding of the way the crisis developed and the study has shown the lengths to which the bishop was prepared to go at that time to suppress opposition to his hitherto unchallenged rule. The subsequent course of the dispute in the county was marked by the enmity that had developed in those years between the bishop and his clergy on the one hand, and Hayden and his supporters on the other, an enmity that grew and festered as the dispute developed.

The Parnell split provided Hayden with the perfect pretext to re-enter the political arena and settle old scores with the bishop who had discouraged the faithful from reading his newspaper and deprived him of a platform on the town commissioners to further his political ambitions. The *Examiner* duly became the propaganda organ of the Parnellites and as such was a particular focus of clerical anger, being particularly detested by the bishop for its abuse of his clergy and its undermining of their authority. Despite repeated efforts by the bishop to curtail its influence, which included assisting in the establishment of a rival newspaper, the *Examiner* survived against all the odds. This was, in no small part, due to the support of influential Protestants, a factor that can only have intensified the animosity between the bishop and clergy and Hayden and his followers. Indeed, the vital role of Protestants in providing support to the Parnellites nationally was acknowledged by a Dublin Parnellite MP, William Field, who, speaking of their opponents, stated: 'They made social and business matters so bitter that I believe at the time it would have been impossible for us to live in Ireland but for the presence of a large number of Protestants in the community'.[1]

Except for a short period early on in the dispute, the bishop and his clerical and lay allies enjoyed the upper hand and the Parnellites struggled to counter the resources of clerical manpower which the Church deployed in its campaign. They found it difficult to counter its assertion that the question of Parnell's leadership was not just a political issue but a religious issue also, in which the faithful were obliged to take account of the teaching of their Church. While the Parnellites enjoyed a healthy level of support in the towns, they struggled to make an impact in the rural areas, where the majority of the population lived and where clerical influence went largely unchallenged. Although the available evidence is sparse, this urban support in Mullingar contained a substantial business element as well as some at least of the Protestant population, although significantly it did not include the labour organizations that were solidly anti-Parnellite. The results of successive local elections demonstrated this continuing level of Parnellite support although it did not count for much when the 1892 general election came around and they were soundly trounced in both county divisions. The result merely confirmed what was already apparent by that time – that Parnellism in Westmeath was no match for a Church and political establishment that mobilized all its resources to destroy it. This included the extraordinary intervention of Bishop Nulty, on the eve of the election, when he warned Parnellites that they could not remain in the Catholic Church while continuing to support Parnellism. The evidence from the election shows that all the communities of interest in the county were split in their allegiance, with perhaps the farming community the most solidly anti-Parnellite, while the population of the towns were the most ardent Parnellite supporters.

While the election result in Westmeath was clear-cut, in Meath in contrast, the two sides were more evenly balanced. The study can provide no clear explanation for this difference, although Nulty's decisive action in relation to the Haydenite rebellion in Mullingar in the years before the split may have been an important factor in curtailing opposition to his authority in Westmeath, once the Parnell crisis broke.

For the bishop and his clergy, their victory came at a cost, both in the shape of a disaffected minority of Catholics and also in the criticism with which Nulty in particular had to grapple with in the remaining years of his life. He faced criticism on two fronts: his treatment of the *Examiner* and his intervention in the election. Notwithstanding the criticism, he was not prepared to concede any ground to his opponents. His renewal in 1894 of his earlier ban on the *Examiner* and the Vatican's dismissal of an appeal Hayden had made to Rome challenging the ban, ruled out any hope of reconciliation between himself and his arch-rival. Hayden, however, had one crucial advantage over the bishop; he was still a young man and could afford to bide his time. When the dust settled, following the death of Nulty and the re-unification of the IPP, he re-emerged as a leading player not just in local politics but on the parliamentary stage as well. His participation, therefore, with his erstwhile opponents in the local political organizations, after the death of Nulty in 1898 and the reunification of the party in 1900, was acknowledgment that his battle with the bishop had not been in vain. Hayden and his followers finally achieved the freedom to think and act as they saw fit in local politics and the clergy were relegated to a secondary role in the reunited nationalist movement, which was now dominated to a much greater degree by Catholic middle-class laymen. If the Parnell split in Westmeath changed the political landscape it left also in its wake a trail of destruction in terms of its divisive effects on local communities, which Hayden vividly described in his memoir many years later. This human cost, epitomized by the deeply personal nature of the dispute between Hayden and Nulty, remains perhaps the most enduring legacy of the Parnell split, not just in Westmeath, but in the country in general.

Notes

ABBREVIATIONS

CBS   Crime Branch Special
DICS   District Inspector – Crime Special
GAA   Gaelic Athletic Association
HC   House of Commons
INF   Irish National Federation
INL   Irish National League
IPP   Irish Parliamentary Party
IRB   Irish Republican Brotherhood
MP   Member of Parliament
NAI   National Archives of Ireland
NLI   National Library of Ireland
RIC   Royal Irish Constabulary
UIL   United Irish League

INTRODUCTION

1   A.C. Murray, 'Nationality and local politics in late nineteenth-century Ireland: the case of county Westmeath', *Irish Historical Studies*, 25:98 (1986), 144–58; David Lawlor, *Divine right? The Parnell split in Meath* (Cork, 2007); See also Catherine Fox, 'John P. Hayden and the Westmeath Examiner' in Seamus O'Brien (ed.), *A town in transition; post-Famine Mullingar* (n.p., 2007).

2   *Census of Ireland, 1891*, 311 [C.6780], HC, 1892, xc.1, 357; A farm of £15 rateable valuation was equivalent to a holding of around 30 acres.

3   *Census of Ireland, 1891*, 16 [C.6780], HC, 1892, xc.1, 32; Grazing farms were in general much larger than the average holding; typically, from 400 to 600 acres. See Paul Bew, *Conflict and conciliation in Ireland, 1890–1910* (Oxford, 1987), p. 8.

4   *Census of Ireland, 1891*, 166 [C.6780], HC, 1892, xc.1, 212.

5   In 1891, the proportion of men in Westmeath 20 years and over who had never married was 51% while the equivalent figure for women was 38%. See *Census of Ireland, 1891*, 354 [C.6780], HC, 1892, xc.1, 400.

6   *Census of Ireland, 1891*, 446 [C.6780], HC, 1892, xc.1, 492.

7   *Census of Ireland, 1891, Province of Leinster, 908–10* [C.6515], HC, 1892, xcv.1, 927–30.

8   Athlone town was divided in two by the river Shannon, with only the eastern part within Co. Westmeath. Neither part of the town was in the Catholic diocese of Meath; while the western part was in the diocese of Elphin, the eastern part was in the diocese of Ardagh and Clonmacnois. See Jim Lenehan, *Politics and society in Athlone, 1830–1885: a rotten borough* (Dublin, 1999), p. 9.

9   Virginia Crossman, *The Poor Law in Ireland, 1838–1948* (n.p., 2006), p. 1.

10 *Census of Ireland, 1891, 86* [C.6780], HC, 1892, xc.1, 112.

11 The town housed large military and police establishments and was the location also of a district lunatic asylum, county infirmary and union workhouse.

12 Newspapers referenced in this study are available on microfilm in the National Library of Ireland (NLI) and some can also be accessed through commercial online archives, such as www.irishnewsarchive.com and www.irishtimes.com/archive.

13 The proportion of the population in Westmeath aged five years of age and over who could read and write increased from 60% in 1881 to 71% in 1891. See *Census of Ireland, 1891, Part ii, General Report*, 475 [C.6780], HC, 1892, xc.1, 521.

14 The *Westmeath Nationalist* commenced publication in April 1891.

15 F.S.L. Lyons, *The fall of Parnell* (Toronto, 1960), p. 120.

16 Monthly Reports of District Inspector, RIC, Midland division, Crime Department-Special Branch, for 1890–2, available in NAI; Divisional Commissioner's and County Inspector's monthly reports, RIC, Midland division for 1892 (Public Record Office (UK) files, available on microfilm in NAI).

17 Lawlor, *The Parnell split in Meath*, p. 22.

18 Alfred P. Smyth, *Faith, famine and fatherland in the Irish midlands: perceptions of a priest and historian Anthony Cogan, 1826–1872* (Dublin, 1992) p. 136.

19 For more views on the destruction of the archive, see Lawlor, *The Parnell split in Meath*, p. 220, and Revd John Brady, *A short history of the parishes of the diocese of Meath* (Navan, 1937), p. 5.

20 Letters and papers: Most Revd Dr Nulty (5 vols, Meath diocesan archives).

21 'The *Westmeath Examiner* and Most Revd Dr Nulty' (Meath diocesan archives); John P. Hayden, 'Impressions of memory: Glympses [*sic*] at the past' (Meath diocesan archives).

1. THE GATHERING STORM

1 See Murray, 'Nationality and local politics', 145.

2 *Land League meetings and agrarian crime (Ireland), Return for each month of the years 1879 and 1880...*, pp 3–4, HC 1881 (5), lxxvii, 795–6.

3 *Westmeath Guardian*, 24 Dec. 1880; *Weekly Freeman*, 8 Jan. 1881 cited in Ann Murtagh, *Portrait of a Westmeath tenant community, 1879–85: the Barbavilla murder* (Dublin, 1999), p. 23.

4 See Murtagh, *Portrait of a Westmeath tenant community, 1879–85*.

5 See Lawlor, *The Parnell split in Meath*, p. 9.

6 Thomas Nulty, *Back to the land* (Melbourne, 1939), pp 25, 33.

7 Ibid., p. 4.

8 Gabriel Flynn, 'Bishop Thomas Nulty and the Irish land question, Part I: 1866–1879', *Ríocht na Midhe*, 7 (1984), 24.

9 P.J. Markham in his preface to the 1939 edition of *Back to the land* (published by the Henry George Foundation) assumed Nulty's statement as meaning that the rents collected from the occupiers of the land would be used to defray the costs of social services. It is hard to see that this could be regarded as anything other than nationalization of the land. See Thomas Nulty, *Back to the land* (Melbourne, 1939), p. 11.

10 *Westmeath Examiner*, 6 Oct. 1888.

11 Conor Cruise O'Brien, *Parnell and his party, 1880–1890* (rep., London, 1968), p. 133.

12 *Westmeath Examiner*, 17 Oct. 1885.

13 Printed annual returns of outrages reported to the Constabulary Office, 1879–87 (NAI, CSO/ICR/2, pp. 28–29/46–47).

14 Brian Walker (ed.), *Parliamentary election results in Ireland, 1801–1922* (Dublin, 1978), pp 251–2, 320 and 379–80.

15 *Westmeath Examiner*, 21 Feb. 1885.

16 Hayden, 'Impressions of memory', p. 30; *Westmeath Examiner*, 23 Nov. 1883.

17 *Westmeath Examiner*, 23 Sept. 1882.

18 *Westmeath Examiner*, 6, 13 Feb. 1886; Murray, 'Nationality and local politics', p. 147.

19 *Irish Times*, 29 May 1888.

20 *Westmeath Guardian*, 10 Sept. 1886.

21 Secret societies, Register of suspects ... 1890–8 (NAI, CO904/18, p. 990, microfilm, ref: MFA 54/8).

22 *Nation*, 17 Oct. 1885.

23 J.H. Whyte, 'The influence of the Catholic clergy on elections in nineteenth-century Ireland', *English Historical Review*, 75:295 (1960), 254–5; In the general election of 1886, which took place just seven months after the previous election, both Tuite and Sullivan were returned unopposed.

24 *Westmeath Examiner*, 11 July 1885.

25 *Westmeath Examiner*, 27 Feb. 1886.

26 Frank Callanan, *T.M. Healy* (Cork, 1996), p. 159.

27 *Westmeath Guardian*, 12 Feb. 1886.

28 *Westmeath Examiner*, 18 Dec. 1886.

29 Murray, 'Nationality and local politics', 148.

30 *Westmeath Examiner*, 11 Dec. 1886.

31 *Freeman's Journal*, 8 May 1888.

32 Letter from Archbishop Walsh to Archbishop Kirby, rector of the Irish College, Rome, 3 July 1888, included in P.J. Corish (ed.), 'Irish College, Rome: Kirby papers: guide to material of public and political interest, 1884–1894 with addenda, 1852–1878', *Archivium Hibernicum*, 32 (1974), 16.

33 *Westmeath Examiner*, 10 Sept. 1887.

34 *Westmeath Examiner*, 20 Jan. 1883.

35 *Nation*, 8 Oct. 1887.

36 *Westmeath Examiner*, 22, 29 Oct. 1887.

37 *Westmeath Examiner*, 10 Dec. 1887.

38 *Westmeath Guardian*, 30 Dec. 1887; *Westmeath Examiner*, 31 Dec. 1887.

39 Murray, 'Nationality and local politics', 149; Nulty had endorsed Tuite's candidature for the 1885 election. See *Nation*, 17 Oct. 1885.

40 *Westmeath Examiner*, 31 Dec. 1887.

41 Hayden quotes the bishop's 'edict', in a letter addressed [by him] to the *Westmeath Examiner* from Tullamore jail, 17 Apr. 1888, reproduced in 'The *Westmeath Examiner* and Dr Nulty'.

42 Letter from M.J. Halton to Archbishop Logue, 17 Apr. 1888, reproduced in 'The *Westmeath Examiner* and Dr Nulty'.

43 Letter from Archbishop Logue to M.J. Halton, 29 May 1888, reproduced in 'The *Westmeath Examiner* and Dr Nulty'.

44 'Address to Most Revd Dr Nulty by his parishioners, deprecating the false and insulting attacks made against him and the priests of Mullingar in the *Westmeath Examiner*, followed by his lordship's … reply' in 'Letters and papers, Dr Nulty', p. i.

45 Ibid.

46 *Westmeath Examiner*, 8 Sept. 1888.

47 *Westmeath Examiner*, 20 Oct. 1888.

48 *Irish Times*, 29 May 1888; the Local Government board was responsible for the oversight of the local government bodies.

49 *Westmeath Examiner*, 30 June 1888, 12 Oct. 1889.

50 Lord Fredrick Cavendish the Irish Chief Secretary and the permanent Under-Secretary Thomas Henry Burke were assassinated in the Phoenix Park, Dublin, in May 1882 by the Invincibles, a politically motivated secret organization, also believed to be implicated in the Barbavilla murder which took place just over a month earlier. See Murtagh, *Portrait of a Westmeath tenant community, 1879–85*.

51 F.S.L. Lyons, *Charles Stewart Parnell* (London, 1977), p. 463; Parnell assured T.P. Gill (an IPP MP), in a letter dated 31 Dec. 1889, that 'this new trial will leave no discredit upon my character or name' (NLI, MS 13506 (2), T.P. Gill papers).

52 *Westmeath Examiner*, 8 Mar. 1890.

53 Ibid., 18 Oct. 1890.

54 *Freeman's Journal*, 17, 18 Nov. 1890.

55 *Westmeath Examiner*, 22 Nov. 1890.

56 *Freeman's Journal*, 21 Nov. 1890.

2. A FIGHT TO THE FINISH

1 Whyte, 'The influence of the Catholic clergy on elections in nineteenth-century Ireland', 257.

2 *Weekly Irish Times*, 21 Mar. 1891.

3 *Athlone Times*, 6 Dec. 1890.

4 *Westmeath Nationalist*, 11 Jun. 1891.

5 *Freeman's Journal*, 5 Dec. 1890.

6 *Nation*, 16 May 1891; *National Press*, 27 May 1891.

7 Minutes of Mullingar Union board of guardians, 4 Dec. 1890 (Westmeath County Library, Mullingar, microfilm BG I26/1/66); *Westmeath Examiner, 6*, 13 Dec. 1890; Revd R.J. Kelsh letter to *Freeman's Journal*, reproduced in *Westmeath Guardian, 12* Dec. 1890.

8 *Westmeath Examiner*, 13, 27 Dec. 1890.

9 Dr Woodlock to Archbishop Walsh, 6 Dec. 1890, cited in Emmet Larkin, *The Roman Catholic Church in Ireland and the fall of Parnell, 1888–1891* (Liverpool, 1979), p. 237

10 Revd O'Reilly publicly acknowledged the assistance of the *Guardian*, in a speech to the Mullingar branch of the INF in June 1891. See *Westmeath Nationalist*, 18 June 1891.

11 *Athlone Times*, 6 Dec. 1890.

12 Frank Callanan, *The Parnell split, 1890–91* (Cork, 1992), p. 179.

13 *Freeman's Journal*, 21 Jan. 1891; *Westmeath Examiner*, 24 Jan. 1891.

14 Letter from Archbishop Croke to Archbishop Kirby, rector of the Irish College, Rome, 29 Jan. 1891 quoted in Mark Tierney, 'Dr Croke, the Irish bishops and the Parnell crisis, 18 November 1890–21 April 1891', *Collectanea Hibernica*, 11 (1968), 139.

15 *Irish Times*, 20 Jan. 1891.

16 *Westmeath Examiner*, 13 Dec. 1890.

17 *Westmeath Examiner*, 10 Jan. 1891.

18 The RIC believed that all ten branches of the GAA in the county at the time were under Fenian control. See Secret societies, Register of home associations 1890–3: Gaelic Athletic Association (CO904/16, p.281.2; NAI microfilm: MFA 54/7); Monthly reports of District Inspector, RIC, Midland Division, Crime Department – Special branch, for Dec. 1890 and Feb. 1891 (NAI: CBS, DICS, Box 4).

19 Secret Societies, Register of Home Associations 1890–93, Irish National Federation: No. of branches ... 1891 (CO904/16, p.388; NAI microfilm: MFA 54/7).

20 *Westmeath Guardian*, 20 Mar. 1891.

21 *Westmeath Examiner*, 21 Mar. 1891

22 Monthly report of District Inspector, RIC, for Mar. 1891 (NAI: CBS, DICS, Box 4); *Westmeath Nationalist*, 30 Apr. 1891.

23 Minutes of Mullingar Guardians 2, 23, 30 Apr. 1891 (BG 1266/1/67).

24 Hayden, 'Impressions of memory', p. 50.

25 See C.J. Woods, 'The general election of 1892' in F.S.L. Lyons and R.A. Hawkins (eds), *Ireland under the Union, varieties of tension: essays in honour of T.W. Moody* (Oxford, 1980), pp 289–319.

26 *Westmeath Examiner*, 16 July 1892.

27 Lyons, *Parnell*, pp 581–2.

28 Monthly Report of District Inspector, RIC, for Mar. 1891 (NAI: CBS, DICS, Box 4).

29 *Weekly Irish Times*, 21 Mar. 1891.

30 *Westmeath Guardian*, 10 Apr. 1891.

31 *Westmeath Nationalist*, 14 May 1891.

32 *Westmeath Examiner*, 9 May 1891.

33 Revd Drum the Administrator in Mullingar claimed, that except for train excursionists from Dublin, the crowd was only 500, with just 150 of those from Mullingar and vicinity *(Freeman's Journal*, 13 May 1891). The *Nation* (16 May 1891), put the attendance at 1,500, describing it as a 'generous estimate'.

34 *Westmeath Nationalist*, 14 May 1891.

35 *Nation*, 16 May 1891; Lawlor, *Divine right*, p. 16.

36 *Freeman's Journal*, 11 May 1891; *Westmeath Examiner*, 16 May 1891.

37 *National Press*, 1–6 June 1891.

38 *National Press*, 2 July 1891.

39 *Westmeath Nationalist*, 18 June 1891.

40 *Westmeath Nationalist*, 2 July 1891.

41 *Westmeath Examiner*, 11 July 1891.

42 *Freeman's Journal*, 9 June 1891.

43 *Westmeath Guardian*, 5 June 1891.

44 The RIC reported, earlier in the year, that as a result of the split, 'boycotting and intimidation have practically ceased'. See Monthly report of District Inspector, RIC, for Feb. 1891 (NAI: CBS, DICS, Box 4); *Westmeath Examiner*, 18 July 1891.

45 *Westmeath Examiner*, 1 Aug. 1891.

46 Secret Societies, Register of Home Associations 1890–3: Irish National League, number of branches for each quarter, 1891 (CO904/16, p. 208, NAI microfilm MFA 54/7).

47 *Freeman's Journal*, 14 Sept. 1891.

48 Joseph West Ridgeway, Irish Under-Secretary, cited in Emmet Larkin, *The Roman Catholic Church and the fall of Parnell, 1888–1891* (Liverpool, 1979), p. 286.

49 *Westmeath Examiner*, 10, 24 Oct. 1891; *Freeman's Journal*, 12 Oct. 1891.

50 *Westmeath Independent*, 10 Oct. 1891; *Athlone Times*, 10 Oct. 1891; *Westmeath Guardian*, 9, 16 Oct. 1891.

51 *Freeman's Journal*, 12 Oct. 1891.

52 Alan Bell, the RIC District Inspector in Mullingar, believed that Parnell's death had 'increased the bitterness and widened the split between the two parties'. See Monthly Report of District Inspector, RIC, for Oct. 1891 (NAI: CBS, DICS, Box 4).

3. THE VERDICT OF THE PEOPLE

1 *Westmeath Examiner*, 17 Oct. 1891.

2 Ibid.

3 Protestants comprised 17% of the population of Mullingar in 1891 with the

Nationalist claiming that up to 50 (Tories) were included on the town's electoral roll, which numbered around 230 electors. See *Census of Ireland, 1891, 461* [C.6780], HC, 1892, xc.1, 507; *Westmeath Nationalist*, 22 Oct. 1891.

4 *Athlone Times*, 31 Oct. 1891.

5 *Westmeath Nationalist*, 30 Apr. 1891; *Westmeath Guardian*, 21 Nov. 1890.

6 *Westmeath Examiner*, 23 Jan. 1892.

7 *Westmeath Examiner, 26 Dec. 1891.

8 *Westmeath Examiner*, 15 Oct. 1892.

9 Marie Louise Legg, *Newspapers and nationalism: the Irish provincial press, 1850–1892* (Dublin, 1999), p. 127; *Westmeath Nationalist*, 4 June 1891.

10 *Freeman's Journal*, 22 Jan. 1892.

11 Monthly Report of Divisional Commissioner, RIC, Midland Division, for Jan. 1892 (CO904/60: p. 12, NAI: MFA 54/24).

12 Ibid., Mar. 1892, pp 59–60.

13 *Westmeath Examiner*, 30 Jan. 1892.

14 Monthly report of Divisional Commissioner, RIC, for Jan. 1892 (CO904/60, pp 20–1, NAI: MFA 54/24); *Westmeath Examiner*, 30 Jan. 1892.

15 *Westmeath Nationalist*, 25 Feb. 1892.

16 Monthly report of Divisional Commissioner, RIC, for Mar. 1892 (CO904/60, p. 53, NAI: MFA 54/24).

17 Ibid., p. 58.

18 Murray, 'Nationality and local politics', p. 154.

19 *Athlone Times*, 7 May 1892.

20 *Westmeath Independent*, 11 June 1892.

21 *Freeman's Journal*, 15 June 1892.

22 *Westmeath Examiner*, 18 June 1892.

23 Ibid., 2 July 1892.

24 *Freeman's Journal*, 4 July 1892.

25 *Westmeath Nationalist*, 7 July 1892.

26 Thomas Nulty, 'Pastoral letter of the Most Revd Dr Nulty, lord bishop of Meath; to the clergy and laity of the diocese of Meath' in *Explanatory introduction to the defence of the pastoral... and to his lordship's reply to the judgement ... on the late South Meath election petition* (Dublin, 1893), p. 32; *Irish Times*, July 13, 1892.

27 *Westmeath Examiner*, 16 July 1892. The *Examiner* claimed that Kilbeggan voted ten to one for O'Donoghue, with Athlone five to one in favour; Following an analysis of the election results based on previous voting patterns, the Dublin *Evening Telegraph* concluded that a massive 67% of the Parnellite tally in North Westmeath was accounted for by 'Tory' voters. Its estimate for the southern division, based on the much larger Parnellite vote there, was 18%. See *Evening Telegraph*, 22 July 1892.

28 Monthly report of Divisional Commissioner, RIC, for July 1892 (CO904/60, p. 147, NAI: 54/24).

29 *Westmeath Examiner*, 16 July 1892.

30 *Westmeath Independent*, 16 July 1892.

31 Davitt had been elected for Meath 10 years previously, but was disqualified from taking his seat as he was in prison at the time.

32 *Freeman's Journal*, 29 June, 2 July 1892.

33 Monthly Report of Divisional Commissioner, RIC, for Mar. 1892 (CO904/60, p. 53, NAI: MFA 54/24).

34 Monthly Report of District Inspector, RIC, for Jul. 1892 (NAI: CBS, DICS, Box 4).

35 Ibid.; Woods cites evidence from the Meath election petitions that almost all the priests in that county were actively involved on the anti-Parnellite side. We can reasonably assume that this was the case in the western part of Dr Nulty's diocese as well. See Woods, 'The general election of 1892', p. 298.

36 Monthly Report of Divisional Commissioner, RIC, for July 1892 (CO904/60, p. 150–51, NAI: MFA 54/25).

37 *Westmeath Examiner*, 6 Aug. 1892; *Drogheda Independent*, 30 July 1892.

4. THE AFTERMATH

1 *Westmeath Guardian*, 20 Oct. 1893.

2 *Westmeath Nationalist, 23 Mar. 1893.

3 Lawlor, *The Parnell split in Meath*, p. 225; Murray, 'Nationality and local politics', p. 156.

4 Séamus Mac Gabhann, 'The Parnell split in Meath: an interview', *Ríocht na Midhe*, 19 (2008), 191.

5 Dr Nulty pastoral letter (1894), p. 3 in 'Letters and papers, Dr Nulty', ii; Interview with Nicholas Nally (who succeeded J.P. Hayden as editor of the *Examiner*), 11 Oct. 1999, cited in Michael

Wheatley, *Nationalism and the Irish party: provincial Ireland, 1910–1916* (Oxford, 2005), p. 119.

6 Letter to Cardinal Logue, archbishop of Armagh, 17 Mar. 1894 and Cardinal Ledochowski, prefect of Propaganda, 30 Mar. 1894, both reproduced in *Westmeath Examiner*, Nov. 3, 1894; Hayden had previously appealed to Rome when the *Examiner* had been publicly condemned by Nulty in 1888.

7 *Westmeath Examiner*, Nov. 3, 1894; Letter to Cardinal Logue from J.P. Hayden dated 27 Oct. 1894 in 'The *Westmeath Examiner* and Dr Nulty'.

8 *The Times* 31 Oct. 1894: *Irish Daily Independent* report of 29 Oct. 1894, reproduced in the *Westmeath Examiner*, 3 Nov. 1894.

9 *Westmeath Nationalist*, 29 Nov. 1894; *The Times*, 24 Nov. 1894.

10 Hayden maintained that the *Nationalist*, which he dubbed the 'Palace organ', was under the control of the clergy and that Nulty was a director of the paper. These claims were denied by the *Nationalist* but given substance by police intelligence reports. See *Westmeath Examiner*, 3 Nov. 1894 and Monthly Report of District Inspector, RIC, for Apr. 1892 (NAI: CBS, DICS, Box 4).

11 Nulty, 'Pastoral letter of Dr Nulty', pp 16, 32, 33

12 Michael Davitt, 'The priest in politics', *Nineteenth Century*, 33 (Jan. 1893), cited in Lawlor, *The Parnell split in Meath*, p.144.

13 Nulty, 'Pastoral letter of Dr Nulty', p. 33.

14 'Address to Most Revd Dr Nulty ... followed by his ... reply' in 'Letters and papers, Dr Nulty', i.

15 Nulty, 'Pastoral letter of Dr Nulty', p. 25.

16 *Freeman's Journal*, 1 Jan. 1896; Following the 1892 election the anti-Parnellite side itself divided into two factions: one led by Tim Healy – which had the support of the majority of the clergy – and the other led by John Dillon.

17 *Westmeath Examiner*, 31 Oct. 1896.

18 *Westmeath Examiner*, 19 & 31 Sept. 1896.

19 Paul Rouse, 'Hayden, John Patrick' in James McGuire and James Quinn (eds), *Dictionary of Irish biography* (Cambridge, 2009), http://dib.cambridge.org, accessed 7 Apr. 2017.

20 The clergy enjoyed one last success in the general election of 1900, when the Healyite candidate for North Westmeath, Patrick Kennedy, defeated Ginnell, the official UIL candidate, by 1,763 votes to 1,418.

21 *Westmeath Examiner*, 6 Jan. 1906.

22 Hayden, 'Impressions of memory', p.47.

CONCLUSION

1 *Irish Weekly Independent*, 8 Feb. 1896, cited in Paul Bew, *Conflict and conciliation in Ireland, 1890–1910* (Oxford, 1995), p. 21.